# THE LEARNING-DISABLED CHILD: WAYS THAT PARENTS CAN HELP

# THE LEARNING-DISABLED CHILD: WAYS THAT PARENTS CAN HELP

SUZANNE H. STEVENS

JOHN F. BLAIR, Publisher
Winston-Salem, North Carolina

*Seventh Printing, 1991*

**Library of Congress Cataloging in Publication Data**

Stevens, Suzanne H        1938–
   The learning-disabled child.

   Bibliography: p.
   Includes index.
   1.  Problem children.  2.  Learning disabilities.
3.  Children—Management.  I.  Title.
HQ773.S66        649'.15        79–26941
ISBN 0–89587–013–4
ISBN 0–89587–014–2 pbk.

To Hank
and all the LD children
who have taught me so much

———————

# Preface

FOR PARENTS OF LEARNING-DISABLED CHIL-
dren, there are five kinds of books on the market:

1. Inspirational books. Famous men of tremendous talent
who succeeded despite their learning disabilities are held up as
examples. These biographies are designed to encourage the LD
child and his parents to take heart.

2. Teach-him-yourself-at-home books. These sell like those
well-known hot cakes. The parents of LD children are desperate—they'll try anything! A lot of authors (most of them
well-meaning, some of them out-and-out quacks) make a great
deal of money writing workbooks and home reading-improve-
ment courses that are of no help to LD children.

3. Scholarly presentations by highly trained professionals.
Some of these would be helpful if parents could only understand them. Most of these books, however, present findings and
theories of such a highly technical nature that they are of little
value to parents.

4. Success stories. Usually these are biographies written by
LD teachers or mothers of LD children. "My son didn't learn
to read until he was twelve years old and now he's a brain surgeon." It's never "My son the plumber . . . " or "My son the drug
store clerk . . . " The main character is invariably a great success.
Such stories are an inspiration to others. And that's good. But
not all LD children grow up to be great successes. Most will
blend into society as just average people.

5. Dire-warnings-of-what-can-happen books. Prisons and
welfare roles are filled with the learning-disabled. It's important
to hear their stories. It's frightening to see the figures that tell

what becomes of children who fail in school. Such books arouse public interest. They point out the fact that learning-disabled children don't merely need help—they *must* have it.

None of the books ever seem to talk about LD people who are just plain okay. And there are many of those people.

Whether they're learning-disabled or not, most youngsters are not going to grow up to be judges, brain surgeons, or senators. Every minority group (and to be learning-disabled is to be part of a minority) has its outstanding successes. We need the encouragement we get from those examples. But most of us grow up to be ordinary. We find pleasure and satisfaction in just being "normal." We can cope—we live, we love, we enjoy —and we're okay.

The object of this book is to help parents raise their learning-disabled children so that they, too, can grow up to be okay— so that they will be happy, well-adjusted, and normally successful adults despite their learning disabilities.

# Contents

# Note to the Reader

IN THIS BOOK, THE PRONOUN *he* WILL BE USED in all cases to refer to a learning-disabled individual. Doing so is based on fact, not "sexism." Experts produce various figures, but they agree that between 70 and 80 percent of all learning-disabled individuals are male.

Likewise, *she* will always be used to refer to a teacher, a psychologist, or a learning disabilities specialist. Here again, facts support the usage. While there are many men who work in various capacities with learning-disabled children, most of the people a disabled child sees for help—especially if the youngster is in elementary school—are women.

Various forms of the term *learning disability* crop up so often that they are abbreviated as *LD* much of the time. That's convenient and logical, but often confusing. Sometimes it's proper to use the abbreviation, sometimes it's not. And sometimes *LD* may seem to stand for two different terms at once. The following explanation should help in keeping the terminology straight:

Learning disability will not be abbreviated as *LD* when the term is used as a noun. Nobody has an LD. Instead, we say, "John has a learning disability." Also note that learning disabilities come one to a customer. A child may have many different learning problems, but they go together to make his own personal learning disability. Thus, no matter how many problems he has, John does not have learning disabilities; he has *a* learning disability. These phrases are correct: his learning disability, some learning disabilities, a learning disability, John's learning disability.

The abbreviation *LD* may be used as an adjective to indicate that a person has a learning disability; that is, it may be used to mean *learning-disabled*. For example, we say either "the learning-disabled child" or "the LD child"; "the learning-disabled students" or "the LD students."

*LD* may also be used as an abbreviation of *learning disabilities* when the term is used as an adjective. We may say "the LD teacher" for "the learning disabilities teacher"; "the LD class" for "the learning disabilities class"; and so on.

# ·1·
# SOME OF THE BASICS:
## Let's Be Sure We're Talking about the Same Thing

WHAT IS A LEARNING DISABILITY? THERE IS NO commonly accepted definition. The experts simply do not agree.

There are only four points that all the professionals will accept as true of all learning-disabled individuals. These points of general agreement are

1. The learning-disabled individual does not learn satisfactorily from standard methods of instruction.
2. The basic cause for his failure to learn is not a lack of normal intelligence.
3. The basic cause is not a psychological problem.
4. The basic cause is not a physical handicap.

Thus, to classify a person as learning-disabled is to place him in a particular group while giving only a limited amount of information. Within this group there is a long and varied list of types of individuals and types of difficulties. The term *learning-disabled* covers a very broad range of learning problems.

### He Does Not Learn Satisfactorily

A learning disability prevents a child from successfully mastering one or more of the basic skills: reading, writing, spelling, and mathematics. These skills, of course, affect all areas of school work. A general lack of success in school results. But the key to the failure almost always lies in the old three Rs—reading, writing (including spelling), and 'rithmetic.

**Dyslexia** is a medical term which originally meant the impaired use of words. Many think of dyslexia as a reading disability. The original Greek word implies a broader problem. The most accurate translation is provided in the commonly used term "specific language disability," or just "language disability." Discovered by medical researchers in the early 1900s, dyslexia is the most commonly seen and widely known kind of learning disability. The dyslexic child is the one who shows up at school a completely normal little six-year-old. He's eager and ready to learn to read. But he quickly amazes everybody with his lack of success. (He can't write or spell either, but the reading is the main issue.) The poorly informed call this type of youngster a "mirror reader" or "one of those kids who read backwards."

Originally, the word dyslexia described a very specific problem with clearly defined symptoms. A handful of doctors (mostly American and British) did research. A tiny group of educators developed methods of therapy. Specially trained teachers worked in clinics and a few of the most exclusive private schools. (Until the late 1960s, a learning-disabled child could seldom get help unless his parents had the money and influence to get him into a top-notch private school. To a lesser extent, that tradition continues today. The best LD therapy still tends to be found in clinics and in private country-day-type schools.)

During the years when no one knew much about dyslexia, the word kept a definite meaning because only experts used it. But then, in the mid 1960s, the general public became interested in the subject. Women's magazines, bridge table conversations, people eager to make some money, neighbors chatting over the backyard fence—all contributed to the talk about the new fad topic. It was "in" to know about dyslexia, and even more "in" to have it.

In 1966 Mrs. Grisson was having difficulty with one of her four children. Walter, her fourth-grade son, was always in trouble at school. His grades were not very good. He had a reputation as a bully, a fighter, a petty thief. Everybody thought of him as a generally destructive, unmanageable, undesirable child. Most of the mothers in the Grissons' neighborhood preferred that their children not play with the boy. He seemed bright enough, but had a terrible attitude.

Mrs. Grisson took Walter to a doctor for testing. It was discovered that he had mixed dominance (see page 19); therefore, he was diagnosed as having dyslexia. These two "facts" supplied Walter's mother with a juicy conversational topic. Her son's dyslexia added a wonderful element of excitement to her life.

The doctor's diagnosis provided Walter with a perfect excuse for not succeeding, not trying, and not behaving. Nothing was done to help him in school. Nothing was done to correct his basic learning problem—if there was one. Nothing was done to help him become better adjusted.

Sticking the label *dyslexia* on this boy did not help him at all.

During the 1960s everybody thought he knew about dyslexia. The label was stuck onto almost any child with almost any kind of problem. Dyslexia meant different things to different people. It could mean anything and everything. It soon reached the point where the word meant nothing at all.

Some of the old-time experts kept using the word with its original definition, but many of them began searching for a new term. And a new generation of experts was divided over the issue.

Some wanted a new labeling word. They sought a mutually acceptable name for a clearly definable condition. Much new research had been done. The situation had become more complicated than in the past. Many children were failing to learn to read, but they didn't seem to have much in common. Their symptoms didn't fall into nice, neat, totally predictable patterns. For a while, the only widely accepted label for the problem was *reading deficiency*. The term said nothing more than "The kid can't read."

Others in the new generation of experts believed the whole theory of dyslexia was a bunch of baloney. They did research. They studied and argued. They claimed, "Children who are mentally, physically, and emotionally normal will not fail to learn. No one is 'just made that way.' Something other than the child himself must be causing the problem." Their mission was to find those outside causes and correct them. Teaching methods, parents' attitudes, the educational environment—everything and everybody fell under their accusing gaze. Children were failing to learn, and it had to be somebody's fault. They used the term *reading deficiency* and searched for someone to blame.

> In the summer of 1971, I took a graduate course in remedial reading. (The term *learning disabilities* was not yet "in.") The instructor was a young, dedicated, well-trained professional.
>
> At the first class meeting, he introduced himself by saying, "Good morning. I'm George Deal. And there is no such thing as dyslexia."

The word and the original theory behind it had fallen almost totally out of favor, especially among the professionals in the field. And it has never returned to wide acceptance. Some of those who truly believed in a clearly definable condition called dyslexia gradually shifted to calling it a *specific language disability*. Slowly, even this group gave in to using the vague but generally accepted term *learning disability*.

The type of learning problem described by the word dyslexia, a long list of very similar problems, and a whole group of seemingly unrelated learning difficulties got lumped into the general term now used to include them all: learning disability.

**Dysgraphia** is the medical term originally used to indicate a writing disability. Dysgraphia is most often seen as a part of dyslexia. Along with his trouble in learning to read, the student is unable to control a pencil or develop reasonable skill in forming letters and numbers. Most therapists treat dysgraphia as a side issue of little importance. Almost all their teaching is aimed at improving reading and spelling. They merely shrug at papers that are a jumbled mess of unreadable scratches. They believe that once the student learns to spell, the penmanship will take care of itself.

This is not true. And it's not fair to the child. The inability to produce a decent-looking paper causes him much embarrassment. Most people with dyslexia learn to live with their reading problem. But their writing problem is a constant source of agony.

> Kenneth was an extremely bright eight-year-old. He had done very well in the first and second grades in public school. When placed in the third grade in a private school, he fell apart.
>
> His happy, playful outlook on life suddenly disappeared. Homework became an unbearable chore. Lying, screaming, crying, hiding—Kenneth did everything possible to get out of sitting down to study at home. As matters grew worse, he began refusing to do his classwork as well. A normally cheerful and cooperative little boy, he was rapidly becoming a serious behavior problem both at home and at school.
>
> Testing indicated that Kenneth had a combination of dyslexia and dysgraphia. He was so smart that he had taught himself to work around his reading difficulties. He could read well enough to get by easily. It was the dysgraphia that was causing most of his trouble.
>
> Put a pencil in his hand, and Kenneth froze. He could not re-

call what the different letters looked like. His hand refused to remember how to form them. And his high IQ was no help in overcoming the problem. Any assignment requiring writing put the boy into a panic. He'd do anything rather than even try to write.

For Kenneth, the answer was in therapy aimed mainly at his dysgraphia. Other areas needed work. But it was the handwriting problem that was crippling him.

Therapy for dysgraphia is a slow, difficult process. Many specialists let it go because it doesn't seem worth all the effort. Many LD teachers have no training in handwriting therapy anyway.

Dysgraphia is one of the types of learning disabilities that are not taken very seriously. Experts tend to think of it as uncommon and unimportant. Much more study and research is needed in the field of writing difficulties.

**Discalculia** is the medical term originally used to indicate a math disability. Discalculia usually appears as a part of a larger learning problem. Sometimes math is the only area in which an individual has difficulty, but that is considered to be rare.

LD specialists know very little about discalculia. They are usually not trained in methods of diagnosis and therapy for math disabilities. Very few teaching materials are available. On this topic, also, there is a need for much more study and research.

A few of the experts are beginning to believe that discalculia is much more common than we now suspect. It is possible that the condition is not really rare. It could be that it just goes unrecognized.

Linda was a normal, bright fourth-grader. All her schoolwork was excellent—except math. She knew all her basic addition and multiplication facts. Her papers were neat, her attitude good.

She seemed to know what she was doing. Yet her answers to arithmetic problems always turned out wrong.

Linda's mother had been to the school repeatedly. No one would take her daughter's math problem seriously. She kept hearing, "Linda's a great little kid. She's just not very good with numbers. Lots of little girls are that way."

At the beginning of the fourth grade, Linda's mother formally requested that her daughter be tested. The school was cheerful and cooperative. Testing would be done if she insisted, but they felt the mother's fears were totally groundless. The school's LD teacher was called in. Even she felt there was no reason to suspect a learning disability. With the very best of intentions, the teachers and principal talked Linda's mother out of pushing for a diagnosis.

Nothing was done. The situation did not improve. Linda was still a great little kid. But she still could not do arithmetic.

Two of Linda's brothers had severe learning disabilities. In a conference with one of their therapists, the mother happened to mention her daughter's problem with math. The wheels were set in motion, a diagnosis was done, and Linda was found to have discalculia.

No one had considered this math problem important until a recognized LD specialist recommended testing. In most cases like Linda's, the inability to succeed at arithmetic would be noticed but left uninvestigated and uncorrected.

Within these three major areas of disability (dyslexia, or language disability; dysgraphia, or writing disability; and discalculia, or math disability), there are many specific types of problems. Some of these are described in terms of what the child cannot do:

*encoding problems*—difficulty with the mechanical process of spelling and writing

*decoding problems*—difficulty with the mechanical process of reading

*expressive problems*—difficulty putting ideas into any form of spoken or written language

*retrieval problems*—difficulty remembering words to fit ideas

Other specific types of disabilities are described in terms of a particular weakness that causes the learning problems:

*poor auditory discrimination*—trouble telling the difference between sounds despite the fact that there is no physical problem with hearing

*poor visual memory*—inability to remember what has been seen despite the fact that there is no problem with vision

*visual/motor problems*—poor eye/hand coordination that makes copying and writing extremely difficult

All these difficulties, plus many more like them, are closely related. A child with dyslexia usually has problems with poor visual memory. A child with an encoding problem can usually be said to have dysgraphia. How a particular learning problem is described depends on who is doing the labeling.

Most LD children have learning problems similar to the types listed above. It is to these children that the suggestions in this book will apply. (There are youngsters with less common types of learning disabilities. Their parents will find that some of the material in this book will be helpful and some will not.)

None of the situations described or recommendations made will fit every LD child. The purpose of this book is to offer sound advice that will apply to the *majority* of LD children.

### He Does Not Lack Normal Intelligence

LD children are not mentally retarded. The learning-disabled have normal intelligence.

The child with low mental ability cannot learn as quickly as his classmates. If not recognized as a slower learner, he falls behind, gets discouraged, loses interest, and gives up. Many become behavior problems; a few keep trying, but continue to fail. Almost all such failing students develop deep and lasting feelings of inferiority. These children are not learning satisfactorily in school, but they are *not* learning-disabled.

Years ago classes for the mentally retarded were the catchall. In many school systems, they were the only type of special education classes provided. All sorts of non-learners were put into these classes by mistake. Improved screening and testing have reversed the situation. Today it is very difficult to get a student into an EMR class (a class for the "educable mentally retarded") even when he needs it desperately.

> Average IQs range from 90 to 110. (See page 147.) Sharon, a student in one of my LD classes, had an IQ of 78. She was definitely not learning-disabled, but her low mental ability made it impossible for her to learn in a regular class.
>
> The school system I was in at the time had a hard-and-fast rule: EMR classes were available for those children whose IQs tested *no higher* than 75. No exceptions were allowed. Sharon could not get into any class that could really help her. By the time she was fourteen, her life was a mess!

This policy is typical of programs, classes, and clinics designed to help the mentally retarded. EMR programs are no longer the dumping ground for all the schools' non-learners.

The children who are most neglected in our schools are those with IQs between 75 and 90. An IQ in that range is below average but not low enough to classify a child as mentally retarded. A child who falls into that gap is too smart for an EMR class. But he can't keep up in a regular class. If all goes well, he will make about three years of progress for every four years he is in school. From the very beginning, he is doomed to fail because his somewhat limited level of intelligence places him in a never-never land where no special programs are provided.

If such a child has many symptoms of a learning disability in addition to his below-average IQ, he's got big problems. He will never learn to read without LD therapy—but he won't fit in an LD class.

In spite of that fact, children with IQs between 75 and 90 are often placed in LD programs, especially in the public schools. But regular LD children have IQs of 90 or more, often much more. Thus, even in LD classes, these "in-between" children can't think as fast as their classmates, and so stand out as failures.

What should be done with this whole group of children? It's a very thorny issue. They have a right to learn. The present laws guarantee them an appropriate education. But our educational system does not have any niche appropriate for them! Whether they're learning-disabled or not, children with "in-between" IQs don't fit anywhere.

LD children are now seldom mistakenly placed in special classes for the mentally retarded. But they are often grouped with the slower learners within their regular classes, especially if they're not recognized as learning-disabled. Spending years in the "low group," with children not nearly as bright as he is, has a numbing effect on an LD child. Information that he is perfectly capable of understanding is not presented to him because the rest of the slow group could not handle it. He doesn't get the chance to be a part of good group discussions where he could learn from the ideas of other students. His work is watered down and presented very slowly. This is *not* what the LD student needs. It isn't that he can't think—it's that he can't read (or write, or spell, or whatever).

On the other hand, how can an LD child function in a regular class when he can't read the book? Even if the school agrees to let him do all his work orally, he's going to have a hard time keeping up. Getting all a student's assignments read aloud to him takes a lot of time, energy, and money.

The question constantly comes up: is it better to place an LD student according to how well he can think—or according to how well he can read?

To truly fit the needs of their LD students, school systems would have to revamp their programs entirely. In addition to the courses in each subject that are already taught—one for slow learners, one for average students, and one for very bright students—schools would have to offer a separate course for LD students. They would have to teach LD Biology, LD Chemistry, LD History, LD Math—LD everything. It would cost a fortune, and all to meet the needs of only 10 percent of the student body. Could it be done? Should it be done? Is there some other solution? Is there any solution? Under the present system, some very good minds are going to waste. There must be a better way.

## He Does Not Have a Psychological Problem

Learning-disabled children are not emotionally disturbed. No hang-ups or mental blocks keep them from learning successfully. They are psychologically normal—at least until after they start to fail.

The child who is caught up in his own disturbed emotions will not be able to put any mental energy into learning. He will fail in school because his mind is off in his own private world of anger, fear, fantasy, guilt, shame, or hatred. Often the emotionally disturbed child appears to have just another behavior problem. Sometimes he merely seems a little strange. It is alarming how many children have severe psychological problems that are not noticed by family, teacher, or physician. These children are not learning satisfactorily in school, but they are *not* learning-disabled.

It is often very difficult to tell the difference between a learning-disabled child and an emotionally handicapped (EH) child, especially among older children. Their behavior problems and failure patterns are very similar. LD classes often become a school system's dumping ground for pupils with behavior problems. (And EH classes end up with a few LD students, too.) Even a well-trained, experienced psychologist occasionally has trouble deciding whether a particular child's problem is basically caused by a learning disability or an emotional disturbance.

In an LD class of fourteen fifth- and sixth-graders, I had the following students:

Eight children who were purely learning-disabled; they had the normal behavior problems typical of such students.

Four students who were clearly learning-disabled, but who had developed severe emotional problems.

One boy who was definitely learning-disabled, but who had such severe behavior problems that he probably could have been helped more by being placed in an EH class.

One child who really belonged in a class for the emotionally handicapped. This youngster showed no sign of a learning disability, and my class did not help him at all.

All these students had been tested by a good psychologist. Out of fourteen children, one diagnosis was wrong, one questionable. The psychologist had done a better-than-average job of identifying students to be placed in my LD class. It is not unusual to see LD classes in which up to half the students have been diagnosed incorrectly. Some of the incorrectly classified children will be emotionally disturbed, some mentally retarded, and some merely in need of instruction in remedial reading.

Having emotionally disturbed children placed in LD classes is not always harmful to the correctly placed students—though it is very rough on the teacher. However, it does mean that a pupil who can't benefit from the class is taking up a space that could otherwise be filled by a student who really needs the special type of instruction available. Or, worse yet, an already crowded class could be pushed up to an unmanageable size by the presence of non-LD students. (Some school systems do not strictly limit the size of LD classes. Too large a class turns a good LD specialist into a policeman rather than a teacher.)

On the other hand, LD children are often incorrectly placed in EH classes. It isn't a question of whether or not such children have emotional problems. Any child who spends several years dealing with the frustration caused by an unrecognized learning disability will develop some pretty strange patterns of behavior. As often as not, by the time he gets to the sixth or seventh grade, he really *is* emotionally disturbed. But merely working to correct his psychological difficulties will not help him. His failure pattern is feeding his emotional problem. He will not feel better about himself or his world until he stops failing! He needs to learn successfully. He may need counseling in addition to LD therapy—but first and foremost, he needs to succeed at learning.

## He Does Not Have a Physical Problem

Learning-disabled children are not physically handicapped. No physical problem keeps them from learning successfully.

Bodily malfunctions can prevent a child from learning. Some of these are easily recognized. Arthritic fingers obviously cannot hold a pencil. Cataract-dimmed eyes cannot be expected to read a page of normal print. Unfortunately, many other malfunctions are very hard to recognize. Blood-sugar disorders can make a child sleepy or unable to concentrate, but the child won't appear to be sick. He'll look as if he's just lazy. Eyes that have perfect vision sometimes refuse to stay focused—but to parents and teachers, the child with this problem simply seems unwilling to concentrate. Major hearing losses occasionally go unnoticed for years. To those who don't know the cause of the learning failure, the hard-of-hearing merely appear to be slow and stupid. Physical problems have a strong effect on learning. And the list of impairments that can affect a child's ability to learn is nearly endless.

Gil was in my regular fifth-grade class. He seemed to be very bright, but was constantly wiggling, roaming around the room, and asking permission to go to the bathroom. He never got much work done because he never stayed in his seat. He was definitely not learning satisfactorily.

In a conference with his mother, it was revealed that the boy was a bed wetter. On the theory that he would eventually outgrow it, his parents had never consulted a doctor about the problem. The bed-wetting didn't appear to be directly related to Gil's classroom behavior. But his mother agreed that it was time to look into the matter. Gil was taken to a urologist.

The doctor found that the boy had a chronic bladder ailment. Gil always felt as if he had to go to the bathroom. The physical feeling of irritation and discomfort kept him on edge. Fear that he would have an accident kept him up-tight.

The doctor prescribed medicine. Adjustments were made at home and at school to help Gil live with his problem. Slowly, the situation improved.

To me, my student had looked as if he were either learning-disabled or emotionally disturbed. Gil's frequent trips to the restroom had seemed just an excuse to get out of doing classwork. The doctor proved that my opinion was totally wrong. Gil did not have a learning problem; he had a physical problem.

## Other Reasons Children Fail to Learn

Within almost every normal classroom, there are some students who are failing. They are not *all* learning-disabled. Many things can keep a child from learning successfully. In diagnosing a child as learning-disabled, experts check to eliminate the possibility of failure due to below-average intelligence, a physical problem, or a psychological problem. There are, however, several causes of failure in school that are much harder to detect. The most common of these are listed below.

1. Poor instruction. From the tiniest rural schools, to huge, big-city school systems, to the fanciest private schools—there are poor teachers. They are usually very nice people with college degrees, teacher certification, and the best of intentions. But they are *not* good teachers. They are a small minority (between 5 percent and 10 percent at most), but they do exist—everywhere.

A child will not learn much from a bad teacher. A very young child (in grade one, two, or three) can have the rest of his school career ruined if he has a bad teacher and misses out on a really important stage of his background.

The teacher is not always the one to blame for poor instruction. Overcrowded classrooms, poor materials (some school systems *force* teachers to use methods and materials that do not work), a shortage of books, uncooperative principals, horrible working conditions (I once visited a school that had two regular fourth-grade classes housed on the stage in the auditorium!), incompetent supervisors and administrators, too many non-teaching duties for teachers—many conditions can work together to cause an otherwise good teacher to provide poor instruction for her students.

Regardless of the cause, a child who survives a whole year of poor instruction will suffer greatly later on. He will start to fall behind, and the failure pattern will set in. It is rare that anyone ever figures out the reason for learning problems in a child who has such a gap in his background.

2. Frequent or prolonged absences. A child who misses a lot of school, for whatever reason, will fall behind. Sometimes he never catches up. In fact, he usually gets further and further behind because he cannot overcome the gaps in his background. Unless the problem is corrected quickly, failure patterns can begin. After two or three years, the child is ready to join the ranks of other non-learners.

3. Lack of readiness. Some perfectly normal six-year-olds are not ready to learn to read and write. Many areas of mental and physical ability must be well developed before a child has a chance to be able to learn successfully in school. It has nothing to do with smart or stupid—it's a question of growth and development.

> Henry had an IQ well into the genius range. By the time he was five, he had taught himself to read and could do some pretty impressive math in his head. He was incredibly smart.
>
> A psychologist (well-meaning, but using poor judgment) suggested that the parents enter the boy in the first grade a year early. A good private school agreed to the plan.
>
> Even though he was a year younger than his fellow first-graders, Henry could read and think circles around his classmates. He was dynamite.
>
> But he had one problem. He could not make a pencil do what he wanted. He was not learning-disabled. He was simply not yet to the stage of development where he could learn to write. Bright as he was, he was being expected to do something that he was not yet physically able to do.
>
> By the end of the second grade, Henry was such an emotional wreck that psychiatry was needed. Being placed in a situation where he could not succeed had caused severe emotional damage —needlessly.

When a child is not ready to learn, all attempts to teach him will fail. Through no fault of his own, the failure pattern will be set into motion. (This is why many experts believe that no child should ever be allowed to enter the first grade until at least three months after his sixth birthday.)

4. Being turned off. An educational psychology professor once told me, "Every child enters school eager to learn. If his interest is gone by the time you get him in the fifth or sixth grade—somebody killed it!"

By asking the impossible, not praising the successes, showing no enthusiasm, criticizing needlessly, forcing conformity, and discouraging creativity, the adults in a child's life often systematically kill his interest in learning. The child does not find learning to be a challenging, rewarding process of discovery. He sees school as a pointless hassle. He turns off and tunes out. Once his interest is gone, it is very difficult to change his attitude.

### Stick to the Basics

In dealing with all non-learners, the secret is to discover the basic problem, then work to correct or overcome it. It is always a matter of asking, "Which is cause and which is effect?"

If the *basic* problem is a learning disability (and not one of the other problems discussed above), then that's where you start.

# ·2·
# RECOGNIZING THE LD CHILD:
## Quick Appraisals for the Amateur

MOST LEARNING-DISABLED CHILDREN CAN BE recognized fairly easily without the use of tests. All teachers should be capable of screening their students to find those they suspect of being learning-disabled. But parents are even better qualified to check their own children for signs of LD problems.

Fifteen symptoms that often accompany the most common types of learning disabilities are listed below. In reading over these symptoms, it is important to remember five things: (1) No one will have all fifteen of the problems described. An LD child may have six or eight or even ten, but no individual will have them all. (2) Among the learning-disabled, some of these problems are more common than others. Some are even typical. But there is not a single symptom that is always found in every LD child. (3) All people have at least one or two of these problems to some degree. However, unless there is a *group* of symptoms, there is no reason to suspect a learning disability. (4) It is possible for a young child to have many of the first nine problems and still have no trouble learning to read, write, spell, or do math. Only a qualified professional can give a truly accurate diagnosis of a learning disability in a child. (5) The number of symptoms seen in a particular child does *not* give an indication as to whether the disability is mild or severe. In order to determine the severity of a disability, one must consider personality, intelligence, attitude, and many other factors.

Next to each of the fifteen symptoms listed is a one- or two-word description of how often the particular problem is seen. The descriptions used are *typical*, *common*, *not common*, and *rare*. One of these terms has been applied in each case to give a rough estimate of how often I have seen the symptom in my own work with LD children.

### 1. Mixed Dominance—Common

It is considered "normal" for a human being consistently to prefer to use one side of the body rather than the other. Usually a right-handed person is also right-footed and right-eyed. It isn't that he can't use his left foot or eye; it's just that he finds using the right side of his body more natural. In sighting a gun or kicking a ball, for example, the left-handed person would prefer the left eye or foot, and the right-handed person, the right. Normally, by the age of six or seven, a child has developed a very strong tendency to use one side of his body almost exclusively.

Those with mixed dominance do not do this—ever. There are many variations possible, but the pattern is always the same: the person does not have handedness, eyedness, and footedness all on the same side.

It used to be thought that this one symptom could separate LD individuals from all others. This has been found to be wrong. Many LD students do not show any sign of mixed dominance. And although it is unusual, mixed dominance is occasionally seen in those who are not learning-disabled.

Specialists use complicated tests to check for mixed dominance. (They sometimes say they're checking for "laterality.")

If a child does have mixed dominance, it often can be spotted without difficulty.

Teachers and parents should *not* attempt to "cure" mixed dominance in a child. Doing so usually compounds the problem. Mixed dominance should only be noted as a possible symptom of a learning disability; it is *not* something to be corrected. It's simply the way the child is. (If left alone, most children will learn to take advantage of their mixed dominance, or at least to work around it.)

Parents and teachers also should be very careful *not* to be critical because a child with mixed dominance doesn't do some task in the "normal" way. Their role should be one of helping the child find the best way to succeed at what he's trying to accomplish.

Lucy was a darling, bright, mildly LD girl in the fifth grade. She had mixed dominance. Though her lovely penmanship was done right-handed, she was the best artist in her class with her left hand. Had she been criticized for this rather odd hand-switch, she would have been deprived of the great pleasure she got from her success in art. It was strange and she knew it. But she was secure in her faith that different doesn't mean wrong.

George was the fastest man on his high school track team, but he kept losing races because of his mixed dominance. He could never remember which foot to start off with. The other runners were two strides ahead of him before he even got moving.

The mixed dominance couldn't be corrected, but his coach figured out a way around it. When George crouched down in the starting blocks, the coach would squat down behind him and lightly hold the non-leading foot. That hand on his ankle was enough to get George to spring forward with the proper foot at the sound of the starting gun.

It looked pretty odd. Sometimes the crowd hooted. Officials usually demanded an explanation. But his family, friends, and teammates were understanding rather than critical. George had a different way of doing it, but he brought home the ribbons. It's hard to argue with success.

## 2. Directional Confusion—Typical

Many LD children have difficulty telling right from left. If asked which hand they write with, they'll hold up the appropriate one. If asked, "Which way should I turn at the corner?" they'll point quickly and accurately, yet fumble to decide which word to use to identify the direction. When told, "Touch your left ear," most LD children will have to pause to think before acting—and even after careful thought many won't be able to decide at all, especially the younger ones. In a game of Simon Says, the LD child looks like a real klutz!

Directional confusion causes the LD child a great deal of embarrassment. Parents and teachers usually make matters worse by insisting that he could overcome his difficulty if he'd only put his mind to it. A teacher once gasped to me, "My God, even a mule can tell 'Gee' from 'Haw'!"

Learning-disabled adults also tend to be deeply ashamed of their inability to tell right from left. They believe it proves that they are stupid.

Very often this problem does *not* go away. Sometimes it seems to be outgrown, and a few researchers are working to develop methods of therapy. But usually the individual learns to live with his directional confusion and develops ways to compensate.

At twenty-five years of age, Carol had a master's degree in physical education and was highly respected as a coach and teacher. The fact that she wore her wristwatch on her left arm was the clue she used to tell right from left. Carol thought everybody had to do something like that.

In coaching her college volleyball team in the finals of the national championships, Carol's instructions from the bench included many hand signals. In the heat of a game she didn't have time to decide about the words "right" and "left." Her players knew to ignore the direction she named and move the way her hands indicated.

Mr. Smitherman was a successful and prosperous furniture manufacturer. His severely LD son was one of my students. This father had never realized he himself was LD until we were discussing the symptoms in a conference.

He said Marine boot camp had been the worst experience of his entire life. His inability to tell right from left had kept him in trouble with the drill sergeant. He spent several miserable weeks being punished for constantly marching out of step!

By the age of eleven or twelve, most youngsters have pretty well adjusted to their directional problems. But people with directional confusion cannot automatically tell right from left with speed and certainty. Pressure only makes it worse. Careful, patient instruction sometimes helps, however, and usually the person learns to use gimmicks and memory tricks to help him compensate. (He also learns to keep the problem so carefully concealed that no one ever notices.)

People with directional confusion should avoid jobs where they must respond instantly to directional commands—as must jet pilots, tail gunners, and the like.

### 3. Similar Learning Problems in Other Family Members— Typical

I wish I had a dollar for every time a parent has leaned back, slapped hand to forehead, and gasped, "Good heavens, what you've just described sounds like my brother." There is usually some family member who has had the same types of learning problems the child is experiencing.

During a conference with the Nelsons, I described all the LD symptoms listed here, then went on to predict some of the difficulties their fourth-grade daughter might face in the future. I warned them that she would probably have trouble with the foreign language her private school required of all older students.

It was at that point that the realization dawned on the father. Dr. Nelson said that he nearly flunked out of medical school because of his trouble with Latin. As we discussed his problems in school, I found more and more evidence of a highly intelligent man with a learning disability. The doctor concluded by saying, "I've always been a slow reader and in college and med school I had to work a lot harder than everybody else. I always assumed I just wasn't as smart as they were."

Of the doctor's four extremely bright children, two had some learning problems, and his one daughter was clearly learning-disabled.

Most researchers are hesitant to say that learning disabilities are inherited. I won't argue the point except to say that if there is one LD child in a family, there is probably another. In large families, it is rare to see just one child learning-disabled while all the others are not, though it does happen. Every combination is possible. But the usual pattern is for some or all of the boys to be learning-disabled, while their sisters show few if any signs of problems.

Three large families stand out from my own experience. In one family of six children, one of the older boys was not recognized as learning-disabled until he was out of high school, three brothers and sisters had no problems, one of the younger girls had a math disability, and the youngest boy was severely disabled. The same type of pattern was seen in a family of five children: the oldest boy was severely learning-disabled, the next boy was fine, the two girls were okay, and the youngest boy had a disability. The third family is explained below:

The Bakers had four boys, three of whom were in the private school where I was teaching. The youngest child was still a pre-schooler. As the three older brothers entered school, each was found to be more severely learning-disabled than the one before him. The third one required two years of intensive therapy in addition to two years in the first grade before he could read well enough to try the second grade. The father was spending a fortune getting his children to read.

When Mr. Baker asked me to make a prediction about the youngest one, I hated to tell him that the odds were definitely against him. The best hope I could offer was that by watching the little one closely, delaying his entry into school as long as possible, and seeking professional help at the first sign of trouble, a disaster might be avoided. There was no guarantee that the youngster would be disabled, but it seemed very likely that he would.

## 4. Extreme Difficulty with Sequencing—Typical

The learning-disabled have a very hard time remembering a series of things in order. Perhaps that doesn't seem to be a particularly great handicap. In reality, though, it proves to be a constant source of embarrassment from early childhood on into adult life.

Starting in kindergarten or first grade, the LD child stands out as the one who just can't learn to say the alphabet. Unless given special instruction, he is often still unable to say the alphabet in the correct order when he is in high school. The same thing happens when he tries to remember the months of the year. His second- or third-grade class quickly masters the simple sequence and moves on to something else. But the LD student hasn't learned the material, and it's never taught again. Unless he gets the special help he needs, he goes on into high school and adulthood unable to name the months or tell the order in which one follows another.

LD children are usually very much ashamed of their inability to remember things in order. To them, it is further proof of just how stupid they really are. The following example is typical of a scene that took place in my classroom every year.

"How many of you can say the months of the year—in order?" I asked my fifth- and sixth-grade LD students.

Most of the hands in my class went up. Comments such as "Shoot, that's easy" came from most of the boys.

Two brave souls left their hands down and made apologies. "Ms. Jones tried to teach me that last year. Ain't no way I'm ever gonna learn that," Bobby drawled.

"Oh, man, that's too hard," Pete agreed.

"Most of you feel like you can do it," I observed. "Who'll go first and give it a try?"

Some of the hands dropped immediately, and a few more lowered slowly after moments of careful consideration. One hand continued to wave confidently above a beaming face.

"All right, Richard. Take your time. . . ."

Clear, precise, quick—the twelve words were rattled off with pride.

It's always a touchy situation. As often as not there isn't a single child in the class able to do it. I was relieved at Richard's success and openly showed my delight. "Perfect. Absolutely perfect."

None of his classmates seemed impressed. (They were still involved with pretending they could do it, too. They didn't know that I already knew their secret.)

"Who else is ready to give it a try?" I searched the faces of the seven who wanted me to think they could. The boys were no longer making cocky remarks. Now they sat very quietly hoping they'd be invisible.

"No point askin' me." Bobby tossed his words casually into the silence. He'd already confessed his inability and was becoming comfortable with the fact that it was now public knowledge.

Reluctantly, one of the younger students volunteered. "I think I can," Doug said very hesitantly. "Sometimes I get mixed up . . . ."

His voice trailed off as his courage wavered.

I offered, "You go as far as you can. If you get stuck, I'll help you out."

It was as though he'd been given permission to be less than perfect. Confident that he wasn't going to get shot down, Doug began. "January, February . . ." A brief pause interrupted. ". . . March, April, May . . ." He paused again, then asked in a puzzled tone, "July?"

"No—but it does start with a J."

"January," he fired back, then scratched his head to ponder. "Oh, I know. I know. June. Then comes July."

"Right. Right." I was nodding my head to encourage him.

"June . . . July . . . What comes next?"

I gave him the first syllable, "Au . . . "

"Oh, yeah . . ." And he rattled off, August, September, November, December." (If calendars were made by the learning-disabled, we'd miss out on a lovely month in the fall. I have no idea why, but LD children invariably leave out October.)

"You left out the month that has Halloween in it," I told Doug.

"I did?" He seemed surprised. But the clue didn't help him.

"October," I explained. "You know—falling leaves and pumpkins and witches and trick-or-treat. You wouldn't want to leave out all that candy, would you?"

Doug grinned. "Annnhhh, my mom makes me throw most of it out anyway."

All of us laughed with Doug. The tension was eased. Everybody was relieved.

By the end of the hour, each of the boys had willingly demonstrated how much he could or could not do with the months. Except for Richard, none of them could do it perfectly. Three of the pupils couldn't do it at all—didn't even know how to begin.

The session was drawn to a conclusion with my announcement: "For our next big project, we're going to learn the months of the year *in order*. We're going to work on it every day until every one of you guys can say them, read them, and write them—with all the abbreviations spelled correctly!"

The word "spell" struck terror into their hearts. The idea that

I actually believed I could teach them this shocked all but one into silence. Bobby shook his head in amazement, and his eyes widened as though watching the cavalry crest the hill on the way to his rescue. "If anybody can pound it into our heads, Ms. Stevenson, you can." (My name is Stevens, but LD children always seem to improvise with it. As long as it isn't done with deliberate disrespect, I let it go.)

It took nearly three months of daily repetition and drill. All but two mastered the skill completely. Ken was absent so much that he showed little improvement. Bobby learned to read all twelve, and could spell and write through June in order. Each of the boys was delighted with his success. Even Bobby was proud of the fact that he'd gone halfway to his goal and knew he'd finish the task next year.

It takes an incredible amount of time, patience, and determination—but the learning-disabled can learn the specific sequences necessary for survival. However, keeping the digits of phone numbers straight is often a lifetime problem.

### 5. Slow or Delayed Speech Development—Not Common

Some children have a developmental lag in all language areas. They learn to talk at a later age than other children and often continue to use baby talk longer than would normally be expected. Sometimes they lisp, have pronunciation problems, or show other speech difficulties. Such developmental patterns sometimes prove to be part of a learning disability.

A mother once told me: "My daughter was talking before she was one-and-a-half and could carry on a conversation before she was three. My son didn't learn to talk until he was three—and he hasn't shut up since."

In the sixth grade, her son wasn't as good a reader as his intelligence indicated he should be. His spelling was poor, and the mechanics of grammar and punctuation were hard for him. Yet he was excellent in math, science, and all his other subjects except French.

It was decided that the boy was so well adjusted and so mildly disabled that therapy would be singling him out needlessly. He was placed in a special English class during one year of junior high school. From then on, he and his family accepted his weakness with language and made the best of it. Nothing further was needed.

## 6. Difficulty with Time or Time Relationships—Typical

Most learning-disabled individuals are so ashamed of their difficulty with telling time that they don't admit it even to themselves. As a general rule, LD youngsters have extreme problems learning to read a clock. By the fifth or sixth grade they've developed all kinds of tricks to hide the fact that they can't tell nine o'clock from six-fifteen. This problem adds to their belief in their own stupidity, but causes surprisingly little difficulty. They learn to rely on others and avoid situations where their secret might be revealed.

Even without special instruction, most of the learning-disabled do master the skill eventually. But they rarely develop the kind of ability that allows others to glance at a clock and know the time automatically. Many LD adults look at the little hand, look at the big hand, then count it out by fives. Most learn to do it quickly. Some never realize that their method is different.

Other problems with comprehending time are not so easy to recognize or understand. The differences in time relationships often cause confusion that makes the individual look pretty foolish. LD youngsters are often very slow in understanding the difference between before and after, sooner and later, yesterday and tomorrow, etc. And once they do master the idea, they often express it incorrectly.

In testing a very bright, mildly LD sixth-grader, his inability to deal with time relationships showed up clearly. Hal had read a paragraph to me aloud. It was a short story about a girl who had gone to camp for two weeks in July. It told how the little girl sailed, fished, swam, etc. There was no question that Hal recognized these as summer activities.

One of the comprehension questions asked the students to identify the time of year during which the story took place. Instantly, Hal replied, "Winter." But he quickly realized his own error and said, "No, no. Summer."

Most people probably would have thought this a slip of the tongue and of no importance. To the person who understands learning disabilities, however, this kind of mistake can be very significant.

Most human beings seem to have an inner sense of time. We can easily judge the amount of time that passes in half an hour without looking at a clock. We feel the difference between five minutes and one hour. Even though deeply involved in conversation or some other activity, we have a good idea of how much time has gone by. Not so with the learning-disabled. It often seems that they were made without mental clocks inside their heads. Time seems to slip by them unnoticed. Even if they are careful to wear a watch to fight the problem, they forget to use it. LD adults are always late!

Thirty-eight-year-old Kermit owned a chain of department stores and employed staffs of secretaries, lawyers, accountants, etc. Although he was a college graduate, he was working with me to improve his poor spelling. He wanted the lessons and was paying for the therapy out of his own pocket. Yet he was always at least half an hour late.

I was very strict about charging him for his scheduled lesson time whether he was there or not. He cheerfully paid for the hours he missed because of his own tardiness. The penalty had no effect on his habit at all.

When he and I talked about it, he said, "I'm always late. My girl friend is always getting mad at me. I'm never on time for business appointments or dinner reservations."

Kermit believed he had a good reason for his behavior. "I hate to wait," he explained to me. "When I'm ready to do something, I want to do it. If I'm the last one to arrive, everybody else is ready and I don't have to wait."

I made two suggestions: that he face the fact that his lack of promptness was part of his learning disability and not a personality trait, and that he buy a digital wristwatch with an alarm on it.

I rather doubt that he did either.

For the LD child, the purchase of a watch (digital or not) isn't always the solution. The child goes out to play with Mom's words in his ears: "Be back for dinner," or "Be home in an hour." He fully intends to do as he's told. But his inner clock has no concept of how much time that is—so he's out until dark, or until someone else's mother sends him home, or until his angry father goes looking for him. A watch isn't much help because he forgets to look at it, and the numbers don't mean that much to him anyway. Since he is very observant of what's going on around him, he's more likely to head for home if told to do so when the street lights come on or when the news comes on the TV. But, of course, there aren't always events occuring at helpful moments to serve as reminders to the child. A digital wristwatch with an alarm is sometimes helpful, but it's often not practical or is beyond the parents' means.

Two goals need to be set up in dealing with this problem: The child needs to be made aware of his lack of an inner clock without being made to feel guilty about it. He's got enough problems trying to fit in with the schedule of the rest of the world without feeling that it's his own fault when he doesn't. And the adults in the child's life need to help him find creative solutions that will bring the desired promptness, while avoiding asking the child to do something he is not capable of doing.

How do you live in peace with a child who has no mental clock? One very firm policy almost always helps: from the very earliest age, teach the child always to keep his family informed about where he is. (This is not the same as asking permission.) Even a six-year-old is capable of remembering to tell his mother where he's going (and being where he's said he'll be until he tells her otherwise). A simple announcement of his destination ("I'm going to the park") should be expected every time he leaves the house. If no one is at home when he goes out to play, he can get his message across in some way. From leaving a note (poor spelling accepted), to drawing a picture, to leaving word with a particular friend or neighbor—he must make sure someone knows where he is at all times.

No matter what system is used, the LD child is often going to fail to be home on time. His family understands and accepts this. But they should not be willing to put up with delayed meals, missed appointments, long periods of worry and waiting. Search parties should not be needed. Parents should always be able to locate their child with just *one* phone call!

Along with this one basic rule, there are many procedures that can help the LD child live without a reliable mental clock. Large, old-fashioned dinner bells, ranch-type triangles, and various whistles can be used to call the child when he's playing around the neighborhood. (Of course, it is perfectly fair to insist that he respond quickly when he hears the signal.) Many a young child arrives at a friend's house with a note pinned to his shirt: "Please send Billy home at 5:30." As the child gets older, he can deliver this kind of message himself. When my own children were small, it was common for one of their little friends to seek me out when he first arrived in our house or yard to tell me, "My mommy says I'm to be home by six." I didn't mind being made responsible for watching the clock. In fact, it made me feel good to know that my children had playmates whose mothers kept track of them.

Sometimes an LD child thinks up his own way of telling time without using a clock. This should be encouraged.

> Ken, a severely LD twelve-year-old, had five brothers and sisters. In his house, the TV was almost always on. He developed a clever way of telling time based on what was on television. For example, he knew he had to be out the door for his school bus before a particular morning show began; he knew to be home for dinner before the start of the evening news; etc.
>
> I once overheard Ken and his mother have the following conversation:
>
> Ken gave his mother the simple message: "Aunt Louise called while you were out."
>
> "What did she have to say?" his mother asked.
>
> Ken reported a minute or two of family news.
>
> "Does she want me to call her back?"
>
> "Yeah. She said she wants to ask you about something."
>
> "Was she at work?"
>
> "I don't know if she'd still be there now. She said she'd be at the office for about an hour; then she was going out somewhere." Ken shrugged and gave a weak grin. He'd relayed the message, but it didn't make much sense to him.
>
> Glancing at her watch, his mother asked, "What time did she call?"
>
> "During 'Gilligan's Island,'" was his reply.
>
> I'd have had to consult the TV guide to get any information out of Ken's answer. But a mother of six TV-watching children is up on such things. Mrs. Williams reached for the phone with a matter-of-fact "Oh, good. She's still at work then."
>
> People lived without clocks for centuries. It can still be done today!

Many children balk at going to bed on time or at living within other time limits placed on them. LD children are especially prone to this. If adults will make it a point always to give a five-minute warning before, say, bedtime, then strictly enforce the deadline, this problem can be totally eliminated.

Do *not* announce right out of the blue: "Okay troops. It's nine o'clock. Everybody to bed." Instead, give a warning that bed-time will arrive in so many minutes. Then, when the time comes, announce bedtime (or dinner time, or time to leave for Granny's) and do *not* take "no" for an answer.

When my LD class went outside for physical education, I took responsibility for watching the clock. Whether they were in the middle of a football game or scattered all over the playing fields, I always gave them advance notice by holding up the appropriate number of fingers and shouting out the number of minutes left before we had to go in. If some were too far off to hear me, the others spread the word. Then, when I held my hand up to call them in, I demanded that they come on the run. And they did. (They knew slow movers would get no sympathy.)

A few LD people have a strong tendency to dawdle. It's part of their lack of a mental clock. Kermit, the thirty-eight-year-old department store owner, was such a person. It took him at least an hour and a half just to get dressed! He would piddle around shining his shoes, brushing lint off his sport coat, selecting a tie, etc., etc., etc. He thought everybody moved through life that way—just letting time slip by unnoticed. And he really believed others were selfish and inconsiderate when they got angry with him for being so slow.

Eleven-year-old Matt was one of the pokiest children I ever met. He was bright, cute, and eager to please. Yet every morning he got his widowed father and older brother into an uproar as they tried to get him dressed and fed and out of the house before the school bus left him behind. A whole list of solutions were tried. It seemed that Matt just could not be made to move fast enough. Finally, in desperation, we agreed to have him skip breakfast at home. This freed him to use all his time to get dressed, make his bed, get his head straight, and catch the bus. Then, when he got to school, he would go down to the cafeteria and buy breakfast. (If a morning meal had not been available, he could have brought a sandwich and a piece of fruit to eat in the classroom.)

In dealing with the LD child's problems with time, it's usually best to find a way to work around the difficulty rather than meet it head-on. ("You'll be home on time or you'll go without dinner!" rarely helps.) It *is* important to be on time. If this can't be accomplished in the regular way, other methods can be almost as effective. Creative solutions help the LD child understand a weakness that he has to learn to live with.

## 7. Retrieval Problems—Rare

When the main area of a learning disability is in the verbal skills, the individual may have great difficulty expressing himself with words. He'll have an idea in his head, but he will not be able to find the words to say it. (This problem almost always carries over into written expression as well.) All of us have experienced the frustration of having a word or phrase "on the tip of the tongue." Those with retrieval problems experience this frustration all the time.

Children with retrieval problems can't hold their own in an argument, so they tend to punch a lot. Since they can't express their anger in words, they hit.

Retrieval problems in LD children are very hard to recognize and are often misunderstood by teachers as well as parents.

Nine-year-old Norman looked like a little professor. This extremely intelligent fourth-grader was a strange little kid. He had so many social and behavioral problems that he had begun seeing a psychiatrist in the third grade. But the counseling didn't help much.

Norman had already been diagnosed as learning-disabled, but his retrieval problem was not recognized as important. This part of his disability needed to be dealt with before his behavior could be expected to improve.

None of Norman's classmates liked him. He had a quick temper and got into a lot of fights. In addition to that, he was a pest in class. Norman was famous for raising his hand to volunteer an answer and then, when called on, saying, "I forgot what I wanted to say." His teacher thought he was just trying to get attention. So, instead of sympathy, understanding, and guidance —he'd get anger and criticism. Nobody realized that what looked like a bothersome habit was really a part of his learning disability. A great deal of emotional damage was done by those who didn't understand.

Children who have difficulty putting things into words are almost always misunderstood. Since they can successfully take in language (decoding) through reading and hearing, it is hard to believe they are not able to put their ideas into words for writing and speaking (encoding). They look lazy or stubborn. They read a story with ease but somehow never manage to get around to doing the written questions. But it doesn't seem as if they *can't* do the written work.

Teachers are always arguing with me about such children. They express their belief that the child has no real problem with written work by saying such things as:

He just doesn't want to do it.

He's a perfectly normal child and has no trouble with reading.

He's just too busy daydreaming (or horsing around, or drawing, etc.).

He's just got a mental block.

He just thinks he can't do it.

He's just lazy; he does only what's fun and easy.

He has no trouble doing things he likes to do.

He may have you fooled, but he isn't fooling me!

Children with expressive problems are often in trouble for failing to finish their written classwork. As a result, they miss recess a lot. And they are famous for not doing their homework. Since their parents and teachers keep blaming them for bad habits and laziness, serious emotional damage is done. The child does *not* understand his own problem and grows to believe he is a worthless good-for-nothing. But the terrible psychological damage is totally unnecessary. This type of learning disability can be corrected to some extent, and there are many things that can be done to help the child compensate for his weakness.

Andy was diagnosed as learning-disabled at the end of the first grade. With tears and hysteria, his parents sent him to a therapist, put him in a different school, and hoped for the best. After nine months of private instruction with a well-trained specialist, he was reading well above grade level. All his skills were satisfactory. Therapy was stopped. In a long conference, his parents were told how to guide their son through the future pitfalls he would face because of his expressive problem.

They were given the following advice:

a. When Andy is rambling and babbling at the dinner table, trying to tell you about his day, don't tell him to shut up. Help him sort out his ideas. Listen to what he's attempting to say, not how he's saying it.

b. Encourage Andy to tell you of the events in his day. Keep him talking. Give him practice. If he goes to a movie, take time to let him tell you about it. He'll have trouble telling the story in the right sequence. Don't criticize him with "Can't you keep the story straight?" Rather, when he gets confused with the order of events, help him straighten them out with questions such as "What happened first? What happened next? How did it end?"

c. When Andy has a word on the tip of his tongue but can't get it out, show that you care and understand. Help him face the fact that he is learning-disabled while also encouraging him to keep trying. When he fumbles for a word and gives up on the whole story with "Oh, never mind," you need to say something such as "Slipped away, huh?" If he's still discouraged, add, "Hey, don't quit without telling me how it finally worked out. You were just getting to the best part." In dealing with retrieval problems, be patient and sympathetic. Help Andy realize this is part of his learning disability. Remember that he needs extra time in expressing himself. And keep him talking.

d. Help Andy find outside activities that he enjoys. Sports are often a good outlet. But from what he's said and the work I've seen, I suspect that art might be his bag. It would be well worth your time and money to encourage him in this area. Sign him up for some of the children's art classes available around the community. He needs something in which he can find both success and pleasure.

e. Be prepared to fight for Andy against teachers and principals who don't understand. He is *not* lazy. He is *not* stupid. Don't ever let anyone try to convince him that he is.

As he gets older, be prepared to fight for special adjustments in his assignments if and when they're needed. If he's flunking social studies in junior high because he can't write a good answer to an essay question, get them to test him in some other way. He will have to do lots of things that are hard for him. As parents, you must see that he's not asked to do things that are *impossible* for him. But don't jump to his rescue too soon. Let him try before you decide he can't do it.

Both of Andy's parents followed these recommendations very carefully.

The boy has now finished the fourth grade. He is an excellent student in every way. And he is very proud of his success. But most important, he is a perfectly normal, well-adjusted little boy. He knows he sometimes has trouble expressing himself, but it doesn't bother him in the least. Friendly, outgoing, full of self-confidence, he shows no shame or embarrassment when he occasionally fumbles for a word or forgets what he wanted to say. Best of all, Andy doesn't think of himself as learning-disabled. He knows he's a little different. But he also knows he's not inferior.

Every year LD therapists see a miracle or two. Andy certainly shines among all my past students as one such case. But it was not the therapy that brought about the wonder of his success. It was his parents. They got him the best help available, then made sure that he did not become an emotional cripple. They adjusted their own actions to fit his needs. Their investment of time and energy is paying off handsomely.

## 8. Poor Motor Control—Common

Some LD children are awkward or clumsy. They trip over their own feet, can't catch or throw a ball as well as their playmates can, bump into things, etc. This poor motor control in large muscles shows up most clearly on the playground. These children are usually the last ones picked for a team.

Kathy was in the fourth grade before her learning disability was recognized. As I explained the pattern of symptoms to her parents, her father shook his head and smiled. "Of our four kids, Kathy's always the one who spills her milk at the dinner table." She, indeed, had poor control of her large muscles.

Kathy's parents took a great interest in this area of her disability. They left the school work and the therapy to the experts and concentrated their efforts on love, understanding, and sports. Fighting mixed dominance and extreme directional confusion in addition to poor motor control, they struggled to help their daughter find physical activities at which she could be successful.

By the time she entered junior high school, Kathy was winning medals and ribbons as a swimmer. And early in her high school years she took up tennis. Under the supervision of a good coach, she played successfully in many tournaments.

After high school, Kathy plans to become a physical education teacher. She'll be good at it, too. Her gentle, loving attitude could help many children.

The area that caused Kathy the most difficulty has become the one in which she finds the most success and pleasure.

The child with poor coordination in large muscle movement will not necessarily have trouble with fine motor movement. When in the fourth grade, Kathy was awkward at sports, but very good with her hands. She had excellent handwriting, loved to paint and draw, used scissors well, etc. Many LD children are in just the opposite situation. Some cannot control a pencil or work well with their hands, yet are "poetry in motion" on the athletic field. And a few LD children have poor motor control in both large and small muscles. It is very hard for such children to find any activities at which they can be successful in either school, sports, art, or music. Yet, even these children can be helped to find outlets they enjoy. The therapist will deal with the problems in school work. It is up to the parents to help their child succeed in other areas.

Ron was a severely LD eleven-year-old. He was unusually large for his age, and his muscular build made him look as if he'd be a natural athlete. Unfortunately, he had very poor large and small muscle control, along with poor eye/hand coordination and extreme directional confusion. In two years of watching him play, I never saw him catch a ball successfully. He either dropped it or let it plop to the ground beside him.

But Ron was lucky. He came from a large, loving family that understood his problem and was determined to help him. Although he couldn't kick or catch or throw, they encouraged him in his love of football. By the end of his year in the sixth grade he'd had several successful seasons in youngsters' football leagues. He did well in defensive positions where he had to block, run, and tackle. As long as he didn't have to handle the ball, he was terrific.

## 9. Problems with Attention
### Short Attention Span—Typical

The LD child tends to have an extremely short attention span. He will tune into one thing briefly. But all too quickly he loses interest and his thoughts move to something else. A reading book, a row of math problems, a conversation, a ball game, a TV program—nothing holds his attention for very long. He can't seem to stick with any one activity. His thinking is done in short spurts.

### Distractibility—Typical

Most LD children are easily distracted. The least little noise or disturbance breaks their concentration. When they are working, they can't tune out tiny distractions. Most students will look up from their work when someone walks into the classroom. LD children will look up when someone walks down the hall, when a garbage can rattles two blocks away, or when a truck rumbles up some street halfway across town. LD children notice *everything* that's going on around them. Everything that can be seen, heard, smelled, or felt will draw their attention away from what they are doing.

Typically, a learning-disabled child has a short attention span *and* is easily distracted, especially in his younger years. In school, he needs to be in a small, very structured class. Parents need to provide such a child with a study place where he can work undisturbed by noise or interruptions from brothers and sisters. Even things in his line of vision can be a distraction. Placing his desk or study table so that it faces a blank wall is often helpful.

It is usually pointless for parents to try to change a child's distractibility or short attention span. Their best bet is to make sure he learns in spite of those problems.

### Hyperactivity—Common

The third attention problem, hyperactivity, includes a physical aspect. A hyperactive child is physically overactive. He cannot sit still. He is constantly in motion—wandering around the room, wiggling or bouncing or hanging out of his seat, running here and there—always on the move.

Is a hyperactive child learning-disabled?

Some experts say, "Hyperactivity is preventing him from learning. Of course it's a learning disability!" Others say, "If you could slow the child down, he would learn. To be truly learning-disabled, a child must be unable to learn whether he is hyperactive or not."

In this book, hyperactivity will not be considered a learning disability in and of itself. Rather, hyperactivity will be treated as a problem that often occurs as *part* of a learning disability, or as a symptom seen before a learning disability is identified.

Some LD children are hyperactive; most are not. Many hyperactive children are not learning-disabled. They seem to learn successfully even though they're hanging from the rafters. They drive their teachers and classmates crazy, but somehow they learn. Others cannot learn while all their energy is channeled into physical activity, but begin to succeed in school after being put on medication to calm them down. And some can be drugged to a near stupor and still not be able to learn.

Hyperactivity is a medical problem. There are prescription drugs that can be very effective. I do not like to see a child put on medication unless it's absolutely necessary—and usually it's not. Some pediatricians no longer prescribe medication for any of their hyperactive patients. Instead, they recommend counseling with a psychologist trained to help overactive children deal with their problems. The results of such counseling are often very impressive. I have, however, seen a few instances where carefully supervised medication produced remarkable results.

Twelve-year-old Tommy had a very severe learning disability, plus a condition that caused him to have convulsions. With the drugs he was taking to control his seizures, he was climbing the walls and hanging off the light fixtures. His pediatrician assured me this hyperactivity was a common side effect and offered to prescribe another drug to counteract it. Tommy's parents and I agreed that as long as his constant activity didn't prevent him from learning, we'd work around it.

I placed Tommy in the back row, where he could wiggle, bounce, lean, sprawl, pace, stand, or lie on the floor without bothering any of his classmates. He and I agreed that he could move around the back half of the room as much as he wanted, provided he didn't disturb anyone else, he didn't do anything dangerous, and he gave me and his school work his full *mental* attention.

For more than a semester this arrangement worked beautifully. Walking along the top of the cabinets or crawling around under the furniture, he was always tuned in to what was going on in the class. No matter where he was in the room, he was always one of the most active participants in class discussions. He did all his work and was making good progress.

Suddenly, in midwinter, Tommy started having trouble paying attention. He couldn't seem to get his work done, and he was often so lost during class discussions that he didn't even know what subject we were talking about. His mind just wandered vaguely.

I called Tommy's doctor and explained the situation. He agreed that it was time to do something. Two pills were added to the handful Tommy was already taking daily. For the first few days he was quiet and sleepy. He yawned a lot and even dozed off in class once or twice. But by the end of the first week, Tommy was back to normal—hyperactive and always on the move, though paying attention and learning.

### Inability to Focus Attention—Rare

Once in a while there is a child who simply cannot seem to focus his attention at all. His attention is so scattered that he can't tune in on any one thing. The rest of the class may be half-way through an assignment before such a child gets himself together and gets started. Outside the classroom, his problem can be seen easily. He is unable to really get "into" an activity. His mind wanders aimlessly. Right in the middle of an exciting game that he enjoys, he'll roam off into the woods. Just at the most thrilling part of a TV show, he'll ramble out to the kitchen to get a cookie. He may be standing right beside you looking you in the eye, yet you feel he is not hearing a word you say and isn't "with" you. These children seem very spacy. Fortunately, there are not many of them. In the only two cases I've ever seen, medication corrected the problem completely.

The nine learning disability symptoms listed so far are not directly related to school. They can be observed in any setting and can often be seen as warning signals long before a child actually attempts to learn to read and write and spell and do math. It is important to remember that some symptoms (such as mixed dominance and directional confusion) are very significant when seen in an older child, but much less meaningful in younger ones. Thus, it is important to avoid the temptation to jump to any conclusions too quickly. A five-year-old who has directional confusion is not necessarily learning-disabled. The same symptom should cause suspicion if seen beyond the age of seven. If seen in a ten-year-old, it would definitely be cause for alarm.

Many professionals refuse even to test for a learning disability until after a child has entered the first grade. These experts will say that a young child with most of the symptoms discussed above is "high risk" and will recommend an attitude of "wait and see." They do not believe in beginning therapy until the youngster actually tries to learn—and fails.

Other professionals, equally qualified, hold the opposite point of view. Research has shown that very careful testing can be from 82 percent to more than 95 percent accurate in predicting learning failure in children five years old or older. Based on that fact, many believe in "early intervention" or "preventive measures." They recommend screening all four- and five-year-olds, then thoroughly testing those that show real signs of learning problems. By doing this, the high-risk children can be placed in special LD classes from the very beginning of the first grade. Then they will never have to experience failure.

It is very, very difficult to be certain that a given child under the age of six is learning-disabled. However, no LD child should go beyond the middle of the first grade without being recognized as disabled and given appropriate help.

The remaining LD symptoms (listed below) cannot be observed until after the child has entered school.

### 10. Tendency toward Reversals—Typical

Many people think the learning-disabled (or at least those with dyslexia) read backwards. It's not quite that simple. If it were, correcting the problem would be easy.

The person with a learning disability will read *some* letters backwards or upside down *sometimes*. For instance: the formation of a "stick and ball" can be arranged five different ways, to form the letters *b* or *d* or *p* or *g* or *q*. A child with reversal problems might look at the word *got* and read *pot* or *dot* or *bot*. But he will sometimes guess the letter correctly and read it as *got*. In reading, certain letters are more commonly reversed than others: *m* and *w*, *n* and *u*, in addition to *b*, *d*, *p*, *g*, and *q*. In writing, the LD child may reverse almost any letter.

This tendency usually carries over to reading whole words or some of the letters within a word: *was* may be read as *saw*, *lisp* may be read as *lips* or even *slip*. The letters within a word will sometimes be totally scrambled: early may be read as *really*, *usually* may be read *casually*, etc. This tendency is especially noticeable in math, where the child will scramble the order of larger numbers, in either copying a problem from the book or working it: 7200 might become 2700, 17 turns into 71, etc. Not every number will be rearranged. Not even most of them will get jumbled. But it happens often enough to make math very difficult.

Words or phrases within a sentence sometimes become totally rearranged: *Was he really?* might be read *He was really* (or even *He was early*). *He lived in the house under the hill* might become *He lived under the house in the hill.*

All young children make some reversals. That is not necessarily a sign of a learning disability unless the child is still doing it after he's seven or eight years old. This tendency toward reversals is related to directional confusion. It is very hard for the learning-disabled to stick completely within the pattern of reading from left to right. They would just as soon read upside down or backwards.

## 11. Poor Oral Reading—Typical

The learning-disabled are famous for the trouble they have in reading "little words." Teachers are always telling me, "That kid's not learning-disabled. He could read if he'd put his mind to it. He just makes a lot of careless mistakes." It does seem strange that a person who can read *elephant, shrimp, father, mother, Mississippi,* and *Kellogg's Corn Flakes* cannot read *of, who, from, does, he, in, it,* and the other three- or four-letter words that make up most of our language. But that is the normal pattern for the learning-disabled.

At twenty-two, Bob tested at twelfth-grade level in silent reading. When reading to himself, he definitely read well. Yet when he read aloud, he made so many errors that the material often made no sense at all.

This didn't bother Bob. He'd butcher the passage, but still

be able to understand it completely! He seemed to have a mental translator that somehow unscrambled the mess he had poured into his mind.

LD individuals with high intelligence very often become good silent readers, but never overcome their difficulty with oral reading.

## 12. Poor Handwriting and Dysgraphia—Common

Dysgraphia is more than the simple matter of not being able to get a pencil to do what is wanted. There's a wide range of other difficulties involved.

When first learning to write, LD children have trouble remembering what the different letters look like. A child may know that he needs to make a letter g but be unable to recall how a g looks. Without therapy, this problem sometimes lasts into or beyond the third grade. And after the student finally gets a picture of each of the letters into his head, he finds he has trouble remembering how to form each one with his pencil.

> I always placed a large handwriting chart in the very front of my classroom. My fourth- through eighth-grade students could often be seen referring to it. Even with the alphabet written clearly before them, it was not at all unusual for a pupil to ask, "How do you make a *j*? I see it on the chart. I know what it looks like. But I forgot how to make it. . . . Where do you start?"

LD children find this problem terribly bothersome and embarrassing. In a regular classroom (and often at home), they catch a lot of sarcasm and criticism because of their inability to remember how letters are formed. Comments such as the following, often uttered by teachers and parents with a sigh of disgust, are common: "For heaven's sake, you're in the sixth grade. Don't you think it's about time you learned to make your letters?" or "I just showed you how to make an *f* last week. You can't have forgotten," or "Okay, I'll show you again. But this is the last time. . . ."

But most LD sixth-graders wouldn't raise their hands to ask for such help in the first place. They're learning-disabled, not stupid. In asking for assistance, they'd be revealing dangerous information to their classmates. Most twelve-year-olds would handle the situation with this logic: "I'll hide the fact that I don't know how to make that letter by writing extra-messy." The other students probably *would* make some very cutting remarks if they ever discovered the LD student's problem. Getting into trouble for a messy paper is much less painful.

Even those who master recall and letter formation may not be home free. There is one further problem that is even more horrible than the first two. It can be called "stubborn hand." As an example, let's say the child wants to write the word *sat*. He knows he wants to make an *s*, he knows what an *s* looks like, and he knows how to make it. So he tells his hand, "s." And out pops an *l* or a *v* or some other letter he had no intention of writing. It makes the child furious. If it happened only once in a while it wouldn't be so bad. But this happens all the time! The child gets so angry and upset that he wants to jump up on his desk and scream. He can't even trust his own hand! Sometimes the frustration gets to be more than a child can bear. Tears, tantrums, thrown pencils, papers ripped to shreds—this problem can produce absolute rage.

No wonder LD children erase so often. Their handwriting difficulties go far beyond poor penmanship. Their problems with getting words onto paper go far beyond poor spelling.

Dysgraphia is usually just a small part of a larger, more general disability. But the chances are that if you ever see an LD child fall apart over his problem, the tears and tantrums will come when he has a pencil in his hand.

## 13. Inability to Copy—Common

"How do you spell applesauce?" an LD child asks.

The teacher writes it on the board for him, or his mother jots it down on a piece of paper.

Still he leaves out one of the *p*'s, or reverses the *le,* or makes the *c* into an *s.*

Noticing his error, the adult then spouts the standard lecture: "It's bad enough you can't spell *applesauce* for yourself. But when I take the time to write it for you and you still misspell it . . . . All you have to do is open your eyes! Good Lord, Kid, *anybody* can copy!"

Anybody but the learning-disabled!

From the youngest children to adults who read successfully, those with a learning disability have a great deal of difficulty copying anything accurately.

This copying problem doubles the child's chance for errors in math. Even when the calculations are done correctly, problems turn out to be wrong because they were copied from the book inaccurately. For those who dislike math in the first place, this makes it really rough.

It is common for a mother to tell of the awful experiences she has had trying to help her LD child write a report. After hours of struggling to get it all down on paper and getting the spelling corrected, the child is sent to his room to copy it over neatly. For every spelling mistake that has already been found and repaired, he puts in two new ones by making mistakes as he copies. The finished paper may be neat, but it's full of spelling errors again.

Phone numbers, addresses, dates, and times are constant problems for the learning-disabled. Their inability to copy such information accurately causes them much inconvenience and embarrassment.

## 14. Poor Spelling—Typical

Difficulty with spelling is the most sensitive indicator of a learning disability. Many LD individuals conquer their problems in other areas but never manage to become better than adequate spellers—if they become that good. No matter what type of disability they have, almost all LD people are poor spellers.

Several weaknesses come together to cause this. The inability to remember a sequence in the correct order is one factor. The tendency toward making reversals is another. A "stubborn hand" that can't be trusted to produce the desired letters can make it still tougher. And, as if that weren't enough, LD people do not have good visual memories. They can't write a word, then tell whether or not it "looks right."

In reading, there are ways to compensate for these weaknesses; the printed page is full of clues that help the reader figure out difficult words. In spelling, however, the writer is forced to rely strictly on his own resources. Training in phonics and the rules of spelling helps. But only about 80 percent of English words are spelled phonetically and logically. For the LD individual, that leaves a lot of room for error.

Becoming a good speller is very similar to becoming a good violinist. No amount of instruction and practice can overcome a basic lack of talent. I used to tell my students, "You had better face the facts about yourselves. Your spelling is going to improve. But you're never going to make the Olympic spelling team."

## 15. Trouble Getting Ideas onto Paper—Common

Many of the learning-disabled are good at expressing themselves orally. They can carry on an intelligent conversation with no difficulty whatever. Their thoughts flow smoothly, their vocabulary is rich, their pronunciation is clear and precise, and they present their ideas in a way that is both interesting and easily understood. But put a pencil in the hand of one of those same individuals and he can't think of a thing to say. All his ideas dry up. He simply cannot express himself in writing!

The child who has this problem hates to write. His constant whining of "I don't know what to write about" makes it look as if he's trying to get out of doing the work. This is only partly true. Indeed, to him there is no torture worse than actually trying to put his ideas on paper. But his pitiful pleading about not knowing what to say is also true. It's more than a mental block caused by his hate of writing. It's a real part of his disability.

Even on those occasions when he does know what he wants to say, the idea slips away before he can get it on paper. Given this kind of expressive disability added to the problems with handwriting and spelling, it's no wonder LD children explode with rage while trying to write a small report.

## Behavior Problems Are Typical

LD children who are not given help and understanding tend to become either hostile and aggressive or withdrawn. Which child will turn against the world in anger and which one will wither in shame? The type of reaction an LD child displays seems related to his basic personality rather than to the type or severity of his learning disability.

The human mind is never idle. When a child cannot do the classwork he is supposed to be doing, he'll find something else to do. Whether he makes spitballs, wanders around the room, draws, pesters his classmates, or daydreams—he will find something to occupy his mind. This behavior is *not* the problem. It is the LD child's way of dealing with the problem.

In the young child, such behavior problems almost always go away as a result of successful LD therapy, since frustration and bad behavior haven't continued long enough to become habits. As he finds that he is able to learn reading and writing, he goes back to normal behavior. If the child is given help in the first or second grade, he never has a chance to suffer from all the anger and pain of failure. He isn't forced deeper and deeper into patterns of poor behavior and psychological problems, because he understands himself and his learning disability.

But most LD children are *not* found in the first grade. For them, their learning difficulties are only the beginning of their problems.

Parents and teachers are quick to put pressure on the struggling first-grader. They tell him to try harder, pay attention, sit still, quit fooling around, get down to business. In their frustration they tell him he's lazy. The child sees all his schoolmates learning to read easily; he doesn't know how they do it. He figures there must be a secret, but no one will tell him what it is. So he becomes convinced that his failure to learn is his own fault. He feels stupid. From this, two emotions develop within him: anger and guilt. His failure makes him angry. His failure makes him feel ashamed.

With these feelings controlling him, he tries to get along in his world. But very quickly his lack of success in school affects everything and everybody around him. Teachers always have names for their reading groups: the blue birds, the cardinals, the robins, the sparrows. No matter how careful they are to hide the fact with cute names or numbers, their students all know which group is the low one. Being in the low group hurts;

being unsuccessful in the low group hurts even more. Classmates tease. They make fun of the failing LD child because he just can't seem to do anything right.

Unfortunately, word spreads. It isn't long before the LD child's playmates in the neighborhood start picking on him. Once it is known that he can't read the baby books with the big print, spell his name, or write the alphabet, stories of his disasters in school spread among his friends. They laugh at him. He either comes running home in tears, or starts getting into fights, or changes his friends (often taking up with younger children who don't know what's going on in his school), or quits playing with other children altogether.

Two parts of the child's life are in ruins: school and play. His home is the only hope he has left. But by the middle of that first school year, his mother is in a panic, his father is furious, and his brothers and sisters have started making fun of him. He's already feeling angry and ashamed. From every side he gets criticism and pressure. No matter where he turns, he can find no help or understanding. So he becomes hostile and aggressive, or he withdraws. He either takes on the whole world as his enemy or slips off to daydream in an imaginary world of his own. His whole life revolves around either fighting or hiding.

The further he goes in school, the worse the problem becomes. A few years of this does emotional damage, but it can usually be corrected. Four or five years does great psychological damage that can sometimes be overcome, but not always. Seven or more years of this horrible pattern usually leaves scars that can never be totally erased. By the time of junior high school the learning disability has become so deeply buried under emotional problems that the child is very hard to recognize as disabled, and often cannot be reached.

Adolescents with unrecognized learning disabilities often try to escape through drugs or alcohol. When the world is as black as theirs is, anything that will allow a few hours of pleasure is welcomed. Suicide, of course, is the ultimate out. But it's rare. Somehow most of these teen-agers manage to limp along. They wait to turn sixteen and drop out of school. They develop patterns of behavior (often bizarre) that allow them to cope. If diagnosed as learning-disabled during their teens, they will sometimes refuse help!

Although these emotional problems make learning-disabled children very hard to deal with, they often are the symptoms that lead to diagnosis. Students with behavior problems draw attention to themselves. The child who is obnoxious has a good chance of being sent to the school psychologist for testing. The little LD youngster who fails to learn but amuses himself quietly and fades into the woodwork rarely gets help.

> I was sitting in the faculty lounge having a cup of coffee. As light conversation, one of the fourth-grade teachers told of a funny incident that had happened that morning.
>
> She had a strange little boy in her class who was always eating the cuffs of his sweaters and shirts. Alert and bright, Berry was one of her best readers. But he never did his homework. Fed up with his habits, she'd cornered him in the hall that morning and demanded an explanation.
>
> She demonstrated his answer by shrugging her shoulders and piping in a high-pitched, childish voice, "I guess I'm just lazy." All the teachers in the lounge found this very amusing. We laughed as we agreed that kids will say the craziest things.
>
> Curious, I wanted to see a child who could confess so glibly to being lazy. I offered to test Berry. But I wasn't expecting to find anything important.
>
> The testing readily confirmed two things: Berry had a very high IQ, and his reading skills were well above his grade level.
>
> Much to our surprise, the testing also revealed a very definite learning disability. Berry had dysgraphia (writing disability).

If he hadn't been eating his clothes and come out with that one off-the-wall remark, we would never have found him!

We started therapy and counseling immediately.

Berry's mother called me while I was writing this. I hadn't heard anything about him in two or three years. Her call was to let me know that after four years of a long, up-hill fight, Berry had just received an award for being the most improved student in his school. He had also been given a prize for some of his art work. "He's fifteen now and it took a long time, but he's got it together," she explained with delight.

Berry hopes to go to a really top-notch college and become an aeronautical engineer. He'll probably make it.

Twelve-year-old Ty was assigned to me during one of my internships as a therapist.

Very small for his age, a year behind in school, prone to tantrums and other emotional outbursts—the child was having serious difficulties. Ty was so insecure that he still sucked his thumb in front of his sixth-grade classmates.

I worked with him one-to-one for nearly a month, then went in for a conference with my supervisor. After reporting on my progress with the boy, I concluded, "I think Ty needs a psychiatrist."

With a vast background in learning disabilities and a Ph.D. in clinical psychology, Dr. Yates replied flatly, "Ty needs to learn to read. He needs LD therapy."

I told her I thought she was wrong, but promised to follow her orders and just keep teaching him.

Three months of work on Ty's learning disability proved Dr. Yates right. With every step of progress he made with his language skills, his behavior in class improved. I did not do any counseling with Ty. I was open about the fact that I liked him and cared about him, but our time together was devoted strictly to LD therapy.

Ty's emotional problems were not being solved because we were working with those problems themselves. His emotional problems were helped because he was learning at last.

## Two Side Issues Worth Knowing

In addition to the symptoms already discussed, there are two characteristics that seem to be found in most LD children. One makes their learning problems all the more difficult to overcome. The other is a quality that is probably their greatest asset.

**Leaks and Lapses.** The LD child seems to have a memory that leaks. He can learn something new in class, practice it until he has it down pat, convince himself and everybody else that he's got it, then wake up one morning with the whole skill gone. Sometimes what he learned has leaked out and will not come back until it is relearned. Sometimes he has just suffered a lapse of memory and the skill will come back by itself later.

Because of these leaks and lapses, LD children are "on" one day and "off" the next. The fact that an LD student cannot do his multiplication tables today does not mean he couldn't do them yesterday. And there is no telling what he will do with them tomorrow! Living with this kind of memory is rough. The LD child doesn't understand it either.

**Creativeness.** Most learning-disabled people are unusually creative. They seem to look at the world in a different way. They are more observant. They approach problems differently and come up with unique solutions. Some researchers claim that the reason for this is physical: in the learning-disabled, the verbal areas of the brain have not developed enough to overpower the creative area. LD specialists say that since the schools have not been successful in teaching the LD child, they have not succeeded in killing his creativity. (Two of the world's greatest creative geniuses were learning-disabled: Leonardo da Vinci and Thomas Edison.)

For several years I taught language arts to seventh- and eighth-graders in a small private school for the learning-disabled.

The headmaster and I agreed that the students needed an art program. Though unskilled and untrained, I ended up taking on the project. Armed with thirty dollars' worth of paints, chalks, brushes, paste, paper, and various scrounged materials, I began teaching art.

The students were self-conscious and cautious at first. Gradually they loosened up and began expressing themselves freely. Their work was so amazing that the headmaster began coming in to observe. Halls, corridors, and classrooms were soon covered with some truly fine samples of children's artwork.

In March, my twenty-three art students prepared and submitted more than forty pieces of their work to the Red Cross International Children's Art Festival. Of the works entered in the contest, the judges accepted twenty-four. They became part of a permanent collection that was exhibited all over the world! That's incredible.

My fifth- and sixth-grade LD class was working on a social studies lesson. Tommy was participating in the discussion from a position behind a room divider made of shelves and cabinets. (He was the hyperactive one that I allowed to roam freely in the back half of the classroom.) During that particular class, he often wanted to ask a question or volunteer an answer. To do so, he would crawl to the edge of the cabinets, poke his head around the corner, and raise his hand. Desks and chairs and legs and feet made it hard for me to see him down there on the floor. Sometimes he had to wait a long time to get my attention.

Tommy must have gotten tired of having to wait so long to be called on. But he gave no sign of being unhappy with the situation. He simply decided to resolve the problem for himself.

At a key point in the lesson I asked a really tough question. Several boys tried to answer it. Try as they might, no one seemed to be able to figure it out.

From over the top of the room divider, something caught my eye: a hand—no, a mitten—waving on the end of a long stick. Tommy had his "hand" up.

I nearly burst into laughter right there in front of the class. But Tommy's face was serious. He wasn't trying to be funny. The junk in the cupboards had not been fashioned into a hand as a joke. The mitten on the stick was "for real." Tommy wanted to participate in the discussion, so he created a solution that allowed him to be called on.

When I did call on him, he wasn't even grinning. He just gave the right answer.

The creativity of LD children is a fascinating subject worthy of a whole book in itself. I'll conclude here by admitting that in running LD classes for years, I learned to rely on my students to solve problems. When the janitor was unsuccessful in fixing our pencil sharpener after three attempts, one of the boys brought in some tools and took care of the problem. When a window was broken and the repairman could not get there right away, one of the students rounded up some odds and ends from the cupboards and had it patched up in less than five minutes. Time after time, my students solved problems around the classroom—usually in ways I never would have thought of. I learned from experience that if an LD child says, "Why don't you do it this way?" it pays to listen. If any kid in the school can figure it out, build it, rearrange it, put it together, adjust it, fix it, or make it work—the LD kid can!

Because of their open-ended approach to solving problems, their free-flowing creativity, and their imagination that considers possibilities most of us do not even see—LD children are a constant source of amazement and delight.

# ON BEING DIFFERENT:
## A Learning Disability or Failure—
## Which is Worse?

ONCE A CHILD HAS BEEN IDENTIFIED AS LEARN-
ing-disabled, parents are faced with several important decisions.

First they must decide whether to believe the diagnosis. Occasionally parents feel that a particular expert's judgment cannot be trusted. In such a case, a second opinion is needed.
Sometimes parents are unable to deal with the news that their
child is learning-disabled. They simply cannot accept the ver-
dict. But until the parents accept the fact that their child is
indeed disabled, nothing further can be done to help him.
Necessary adjustments cannot be made in the home and classroom. Therapy cannot begin at school or in the clinic. Gaining
a thorough understanding of their child and his particular
learning disability is crucial. Parents who see clearly what the
problem is rarely have trouble accepting it.

The second step involves the question: "My child has a
learning disability. What do I *do* about it?" The choices are
all but unlimited. Some parents try to keep the disability a
secret or pretend it does not exist; others decide to ignore it
and hope it will go away. At the opposite extreme are those
parents who make such a production of the matter that the

learning disability becomes the focal point of the child's entire life. So the issue is whether or not to take action. The decision must be made.

Very often parents make the mistake of basing their decision on the question: "Should we single out our child and make him different—or would it be better just to leave him alone?" (They are really asking themselves: "Which is worse—freak or failure?")

But that is a nonsense question. The LD child already *is* different. He already stands out. He will be learning-disabled whether or not he is given that label. He can be taught by special methods that allow him to learn, or he can be left to his own devices and fail. But the fact that he is disabled cannot be changed. Parents can choose only between helping him to succeed and allowing him to fail.

Failure, frustration, and ridicule are destructive. A learning disability is not destructive.

Parents are often reluctant to put their LD child in a special class. They hate to send him to a therapist even when the special instruction he needs is provided free of cost, right within the school. They're afraid he will be miserable.

"More miserable than he already is?" the specialists ask. "How do you think it feels to be the dummy of the class? How do you think he feels about bringing home a report card full of Fs? What do you think goes on in his head when his classmates laugh at him and treat him like a freak?"

Yes, we'd all prefer to have every child succeed in a regular class. But when we face the fact that we can't change whether or not a child is learning-disabled, we are left with the question of what to do about it. We do have the ability to change his pattern of learning failure into one of success.

State and federal guidelines almost always require schools to place children in the "least restrictive environment." In every area where an LD child can succeed with regular classwork in a normal classroom, he should be allowed and encouraged to do so. To decide where the child should be placed for the study of a particular subject, two questions should be asked: (1) Is he learning successfully where he is? If the answer is "no," it is up to the parents to see to it that the situation is changed to one in which the child can and does succeed. (2) Is he well-adjusted and content where he is? If the answer is "no" (and it usually is), it is up to the parents to see to it that the situation is changed to one in which he can and will be well-adjusted and happy.

In a regular classroom, LD children are usually teased and picked on by the other students. They are not accepted. As their frustration increases, their behavior problems increase. In addition to being treated as the class dummies, they become known as troublemakers, crybabies, and bullies. By the time they are in the fifth or sixth grade, they have often built a reputation as petty thieves, liars, foul-mouthed screamers, loners, weirdos, or worse. Frequently, they are more than unpopular; they are outcasts.

Yet, when told that they are going to be put into a special class or sent somewhere for therapy, they shriek that they don't want to go. They want to be left just as they are in a regular class.

Those protests should be ignored. Any child who spends a large part of his school day fighting, crying, or pretending he doesn't care does not know what happiness is. Not by any stretch of the imagination could he be said to be "happy" in a regular class. He just thinks he would be even *more* miserable in an LD class.

Just as the parents had to accept the fact that their child is learning-disabled, the child himself must come to terms with that fact. As long as he is in a regular class where he receives no help or therapy, he can pretend he is just like everybody else. Adjusting his schoolwork, removing him from the classroom for therapy, or placing him in a special LD class makes his learning disability public knowledge. He already is different and he knows it. But any kind of real action forces him to admit his disability openly to himself and to others.

This is a very difficult step to take. But it is vitally important. LD children need a great deal of help accepting the fact that, whether they like it or not—they *are* different. Encouraging a child to hide from the truth about himself is *not* in his best interest. The first step in helping him overcome his learning disability must involve guiding him to accept the fact that he has a disability.

Tony had received more than two years of intensive LD therapy. But it was unsuccessful. He could not do any of the regular work in his fifth-grade class. For all practical purposes, Tony was a nonreader.

There was no good LD class available. He had been given all the therapy he could stand. There did not seem to be a good solution.

Tony's parents went with me to talk to his principal and teachers. In the conference, we all agreed that the boy *truly* was happy and well-adjusted. He was liked and accepted by his classmates. He understood his own learning problem and felt no anger or shame. His attitude was good: he was cooperative and willing to try. Except for the fact that his parents (by agreement with the school) did his homework with him, his home life was normal and satisfying in every way.

There was no class where Tony could learn more successfully. He was getting along so well in his regular class that he really enjoyed school. We did not want to deprive him of the pleasure he found in being a part of a class where he was understood, accepted, and liked. Moving Tony to a different school and a new class would have done more harm than good. He had very little to gain, and a lot to lose.

Tony's teachers loved him. With their principal's permission, they asked me to help them design a special program that would allow the boy to learn as much as possible while staying in their classes. We worked together for nearly three hours to plan adjustments that would make Tony as successful as possible while keeping him in the regular class.

As I was leaving the meeting, the principal thanked me for coming. Then he made a very unusual statement. As he shook my hand, he emphatically said, "I personally guarantee that as long as Tony is in my school, I'll see to it that he gets the special treatment he needs. I have a very fine faculty that I know I can count on. They will back me. Until the end of the sixth grade, Tony is ours—and we'll take good care of him."

(There are many fine public school principals like this man. But it is rare that one will risk making such a firm commitment on behalf of one particular student.)

For Tony, this was the best possible solution. But the secret was that he truly was happy and well-adjusted in his regular classroom. Except for the fact that he could not read, he was fine.

Unfortunately, that is rarely the case.

As a fifth-grader, Cal was already one of the wildest boys in his private school. Between his midnight adventures of riding minibikes on the country club golf course and stealing hubcaps with high school dropouts nearly twice his age, he was rough and tough, street wise, and headed for serious trouble.

In school, Cal's behavior was awful. He was constantly disrupting his class, always starting trouble. The other students stayed clear of him as much as possible.

Cal's learning disability was not particularly severe. However, he had such a behavior problem that he could work only one-to-one. (Even in a very small group, he spent all his time trying to impress the others by clowning and showing off.)

Cal began coming to me for private therapy three times a week. He was very honest about the fact that it embarrassed him to be pulled out of his regular class for his special lessons. I checked with his teacher to be sure no one was giving him a hard time to add to his discomfort. I was assured that nobody in the classroom paid any attention whatever when Cal left his desk to go across the hall for his private lessons.

Once we got into it, the therapy progressed very well. Cal was cooperative and cheerful. He teased me because I made him work so hard. But his attitude was great and he was very proud of his own progress.

About eight weeks after we started the private therapy, Cal's mother called me. "It's just too embarrassing for him to have to leave his regular class," she said. "Cal won't be having any more lessons after this week."

I told her that I thought she was making a serious mistake. But she would not listen.

The following year Cal began hanging around with a really rough gang of teen-agers. They amused themselves with drugs, alcohol, and activities such as stealing sirens off police cars. Although Cal did not get arrested, by the end of the sixth grade he had already had several brushes with the law. His behavior in school had become so uncontrollable that his parents were asked to put him elsewhere for the seventh grade.

I don't know what happened to Cal after that. And I'm glad I don't. It's too painful to watch a child be destroyed because his parents don't have the courage to give him the help he needs.

## "Don't Label That Child"

Educators and writers for women's magazines shout with passion: "Don't single him out. Don't make him different!" But a child with a learning disability already *is* different. He already stands out. He isn't learning, he's hard to get along with, he feels inferior, and he's very unhappy.

The child has a problem. The problem is a learning disability. By using the term "learning-disabled," we are identifying the problem, not labeling the child.

### I Have Met the Enemy and He Isn't Me

There is one thing that helps an LD individual more than any other: knowing that he has a learning problem that is *not* his fault.

The learning-disabled individual almost always feels guilty about his failure to learn. He grabs the blame himself, accepts the guilt, and suffers the burden alone. (Parents usually blame the school, a particular teacher, each other, or some outside event such as an illness the child had or a change of schools due to a move. Sometimes they blame the child.)

When a child is not learning, everyone around him searches frantically to find *who* is the cause of the problem. That approach is absolutely useless. The question must be "*What* is the cause of the problem?" In looking for someone to blame, a person must be pointed out as the culprit. But in seeking *what* to blame, the learning disability can be recognized as "the enemy."

As one explains to a child that he is learning-disabled, the amazed question almost always comes out: "You mean it's not my own fault?" It usually takes some time for the fact to sink in. Once the student realizes that his problem is caused by something over which he has no control, he is tremendously relieved. He's still ashamed of his failure, but he doesn't have to feel guilty anymore. He isn't stupid or lazy, as he's always feared. There are others like him, so he isn't the freak he thought he was. The adults in his life understand and are going to help. He can trust them now that they see what's going on and really do understand. Knowing the name and nature of his enemy gives the LD child a whole new outlook; because he can now take an active interest in his own progress, he has a chance to succeed.

An LD child cannot be helped until he and his parents and teachers can look each other in the eye and openly join in his battle cry: "I have a learning disability. I am not the enemy; the learning disability is. Along with anyone who will help me, I will fight it."

## ·4·
# ISN'T ANYBODY WATCHING?
## Why Public Schools Don't
## Recognize LD Children

MOST TEACHERS ARE NOT TRAINED TO RECOG-
nize symptoms of learning disabilities. Even at colleges with
outstanding LD programs and clinics, the regular education
majors are not necessarily taught about LD children.

Principals and administrators come through the same universities and the same programs. They're not taught anything
about learning disabilities either.

Unfortunately, the few teachers who are taught about learning disabilities are usually given instruction that is not practical
for use in a classroom.

> As a consultant to George Washington Junior High School, I
> worked closely with a staff of English teachers who were unusu-
> ally well-informed about learning disabilities. All of them had
> participated in two courses of in-service training. They knew the
> statistics. They knew the symptoms. And most of all, they cared.
> They were a fine group of dedicated professionals.
>
> These teachers wanted to help their LD students. But they
> openly admitted that they didn't know how. Only two of the
> school's students had been identified as learning-disabled. The
> teachers had no idea even how to find the other LD children in
> their school. They wanted my guidance as a professional.

I asked each of the five, "Which of your students do you suspect might be learning-disabled?"

All five answers were the same. Each said, "In all of my classes, I don't have any other students that look learning-disabled." They had many doing poor work, but in each case the cause appeared to be something other than a learning disability.

This junior high had about six hundred students. While experts use various figures, it is generally agreed that from 5 percent to 15 percent of all school children are learning-disabled. Based on even the low figure of 5 percent, Washington Junior High had at least 28 unidentified LD children. These five English teachers came in contact with every child in that school. Yet only two students had been recognized as learning-disabled! Where were all the others? Why couldn't anybody spot them?

Classroom teachers who do have some knowledge about learning disabilities usually can't apply that knowledge to real children. They may have taken a course, or a workshop, or an in-service training class. But there they were merely taught lists of symptoms, presented with interesting but useless theories about brain hemispheres, and told inspiring stories about famous men who were successful despite their learning problems. No one ever seems to teach teachers anything they can use!

For example, teachers are rarely shown samples of work done by LD children and told what to notice. And if they are, they're shown samples from extreme cases unlike anything they're likely to see in an entire career, or they're given samples of work done by children vastly different in age from the ones they teach. (Seeing the types of mistakes LD students make on high school themes is not very helpful to a second-grade teacher.) The flood of jargon that seems to be characteristic of courses in learning disabilities is another problem teachers must overcome. ("Innate tendencies toward proximodistal movement" means little to the average teacher.) And the techniques teachers are encouraged to use with these children are seldom practical. Either they are so complicated that only a trained specialist would be able to employ them, or they require more time than any classroom teacher can spare. ("Give him fifteen minutes one-to-one every day," experts chirp. "When?" the teacher screams. She's got thirty-four other students, at least three LD children, and a very limited amount of time. She doesn't *have* forty-five minutes to devote to just three children. What's she supposed to do with the rest of the class while she's dabbling in LD therapy?)

Parents, LD consultants, school psychologists, and administrators often think this plea is a cop-out. It's not.

Look at a typical school day. Elementary schools usually run a six-hour day from, say, 8:30 to 2:30. Most elementary schools have "self-contained" classes; except during periods when art, music, and/or physical education are taught, the child is with one teacher all day. There are at least thirty children in each class (often more nearly forty). Those children range in ability from very slow learners to geniuses. They may all be in the same grade, but they're working at many different levels.

One year I taught a regular fourth-grade class in a city public school. Of my thirty-six students—

six excellent readers were reading at or above sixth-grade level;

eight good readers were working at about fifth-grade level;

ten average readers were at grade level;

seven poor readers were a year or two behind; and

five very poor readers were reading pre-primers or other books designed for first-graders.

I had to have five reading groups in order to come even close to meeting their needs.

For an hour and a half each day I juggled my time and spread myself among those five reading groups. While one had my attention, the other four did independent work (silent reading, answering questions, looking up vocabulary words, etc.). I spread myself so thin I could barely stand the strain. Every night I carried home mountains of papers to grade. We never had time to do any of the creative, fun-type activities that are usually included in good reading programs. Some important areas had to be dropped by the wayside: the top group never got to read aloud, the second group got to read orally only once a week, and only those in the bottom group got to check their work with me. To work in five groups, we had to stay bound by a schedule and routine. The fun and the personal touch were gone.

The bottom group got most of my attention.

If I had been able to find some extra time, I'd have used it for enrichment with the two neglected top groups. Had some LD expert come in and told me to give just ten minutes a day to each of my five extremely poor readers, I'd have been rude if not hysterical.

I was young, energetic, and idealistic. I cared very much and I wanted to help every one of my students. But I was already pushing myself to the limits of my strength.

Having five reading groups in one class is almost unheard of. But having children reading on so many different levels is typical. In almost all classrooms, the pupils are at all different levels of readiness, achievement, and ability.

The classroom teacher is trying to teach six subjects to thirty children in a six-hour day. Can it be done? On the days when the teacher doesn't have bus duty, lunchroom duty, hall duty, playground duty, reports to fill out, or some committee meeting—she gets her class started right at the opening bell. Into this day, she's going to try to squeeze the following:

15 minutes — Attendance, lunch count, announcements, collecting money for various good causes, filling out forms, etc.
1 hour — Reading
1 hour — English

1 hour — Math
30 minutes — Spelling
30 minutes — Lunch
30 minutes — Physical Education (often required by state law)
45 minutes — Science or Health
45 minutes — Social Studies
45 minutes — Art, Music, Library, etc.
15 minutes — Clean room; assign homework; hand out notices, bulletins, and announcements for various civic, charitable, PTA, or government groups; and dismiss.

That totals 7¼ hours. Getting more than seven hours' work into a six-hour day requires a lot of careful planning and very tight scheduling. The teacher is already cutting many corners. She's already standing on her head to fit so much into so little time. She usually doesn't even get to go to the bathroom until after the children have gone home for the day!

And then some out-of-town LD expert breezes in to tell her, "If you'll spend just fifteen minutes a day with that LD child doing what I tell you . . . ." So the teacher tunes her out. She doesn't *have* fifteen minutes a day. (And she doesn't have just one LD child, either.) Such sessions would probably not be in the LD child's best interest anyway. Fifteen minutes of work a day can accomplish very little even if carried on by a specialist over a long period. Any therapy that is not successful acts to convince the child further that his case is hopeless. A botched job is worse than no therapy at all!

### Incompetence at High Levels

Principals, supervisors, and administrators often prevent teachers from helping learning-disabled children.

Although a teacher may not suspect that a failing student is learning-disabled, she usually tries to do something to help him. The reading coordinator is usually the first person she sees in her search for assistance. This expert is right there in the school, ready to help with special problems. However, reading coordinators rarely know much about learning disabilities. When asked for ideas that might work with a fifth-grader reading at second-grade level, a reading coordinator usually pulls out a few easy books with big print and lots of pictures, and an armful of old workbooks. Handing them to the teacher, she expresses her opinion with a comment like "That Joe Woods could read if he wanted to. Just look at his eyes—that boy's smart. What he needs is somebody standing over him with a stick." The teacher goes away feeling that only a fool would waste time trying to help that sorry Woods child.

(A lot of teachers would give up then, if not earlier. We're going to follow through with the one in a thousand who refuses to quit trying.)

By Thanksgiving the special material supplied by the reading coordinator has proved useless. Joe Woods is still not learning to read. Again the teacher searches for a source of help.

Her next step is to discuss the child's problem with the reading supervisor when she comes around for her next monthly visit. (Within school systems, supervisors are powerful people. They run whole programs and have the authority to hire and fire. They are supposed to be experts in the area over which they have command.)

As far as I have observed, reading supervisors are usually old, experienced classroom teachers. They tend to use jargon and a knowledge of new trends in the field to support their very conservative views. They usually hold firmly to the one-room-school theory: if the child is *your* student, *you* should handle all his problems. Reading supervisors rarely know anything about learning disabilities, and if they do, they are likely to think the whole idea is used merely as an excuse for poor teaching.

The supervisor will make many suggestions for helping Joe. Being well-informed about the newest materials and latest trends, she'll offer to order some teaching aid that is new on the market. From her experience as a classroom teacher, she'll tell of some game or puzzle that once produced wonderful results in one of her own pupils. The conference almost always ends the same way. The reading supervisor smiles sweetly and coos, "I'll send those books over to you first thing tomorrow. And remember: Any teacher worth her salt can help that child right there in her own classroom." Sometimes she merely encourages the teacher to handle Joe's problems herself; sometimes she insists on it. Either way, the teacher feels obligated to follow her supervisor's recommendations. It'll be at least the end of January before she tries to find help for Joe elsewhere.

At this point, any further action involves a great deal of red tape. If the teacher goes to her principal, he'll tell her one of three things: (1) There's nothing wrong with that child that you can't handle yourself (or that a good swift kick in the pants won't cure, or that any of his past teachers noticed, or that can be helped at all). (2) Fill out this six-page request in quadruplicate and we'll get the school psychologist to look into it. (3) Fill out this twenty-three-page form and we'll call a meeting of the school-based committee to discuss it. The names and procedures vary from one school to another, but the functions of these committees are basically the same. A school-based committee is called together to discuss one particular child who is having major problems in that school.

A school-based committee always includes the principal of the school and the teacher responsible for the child being discussed. It usually has two or three permanent members chosen by the principal. In some states it must have at least one member of the same race as that of the child in question, plus one member of a minority group.

To get a child's case brought before the school-based committee, his teacher must first convince the principal that the child is in critical need of such attention. (Sometimes the teacher fails to do this, and the whole matter is dropped there.) After he sees the need, the principal calls a meeting of the committee. It often takes more than a month to find a time when six busy teachers can squeeze this added responsibility into their schedules. Getting a child's case before a school-based committee can become a major production.

At the meeting itself, the student's teacher carefully describes the child's difficulties and discusses them with the others. Then the committee decides what should be done about the problem. (Sometimes the teacher fails to convince the committee members that her pupil needs special help, and the whole matter is dropped.)

If the teacher fails to convince the committee of the student's need, she has no other place to turn. An overworked school psychologist probably visits each school for half a day, once a week. When the teacher does catch the psychologist, she'll hear, "Sounds like something we ought to look into. Fill out the request forms, get the parents' permission slips signed, and I'll try to work him in for some testing sometime this spring." Although our teacher probably does not suspect that poor Joe is learning-disabled, if an LD specialist is available, she may turn to her in desperation. From her she'll get, "Sorry, I can't help you. Unless a child has been through the school-based committee and the placement committee, I'm not allowed to touch him."

(Typically, there is only one placement committee for an entire school system. The group is usually made up of one principal, one regular classroom teacher, one special education teacher, a psychologist, an assortment of supervisors and department heads, and an assistant superintendent or two. Sometimes there is no LD specialist on the placement committee. This group meets regularly to decide what the schools will do to help special students who have already been diagnosed. The placement committee must classify the child as learning-disabled before the school system's LD specialists are allowed to become involved with the child.)

Getting the child tested may take months; getting his case before the school-based committee sometimes takes longer. It is often extremely difficult to convince the various committees that something really is so wrong as to require attention. The fact that Joe Woods has entered the machinery of "the system" does not guarantee that he will get the help he needs.

It's possible, in a city school system of 46,000 students, where we *know* that at least 5 percent, or 2300 children, are severely learning-disabled, to have fewer than 200 pupils receiving therapy from the staff of LD teachers. In order to get help, the child has to be a real basket case.

Sometimes a whole school gets excited about learning disabilities. But school systems even have ways of stopping an entire faculty from accomplishing anything.

At Washington Junior High School (spoken of earlier in this chapter), the principal and his entire faculty were determined to do everything in their power to find and help their LD students.

As their consultant, I worked with them to develop a plan of attack. The law clearly forbids individual testing and precise diagnosis without parental permission and strong proof of need. We could not ask a school psychologist to test an entire student body. That would not be practical. By careful screening we planned to narrow down the field. We would request testing for only those children who looked as if they might be learning-disabled.

The five English teachers had contact with every student in the school. We decided that they would give tests to screen the entire student body. Every child in that school was to be given a silent reading test, a special vocabulary test taken both orally and silently, a spelling test, and several smaller tests that another consultant helped us design. We knew that our screening would not pick out the LD students; it would give us only a first set of clues as to who they might be. We'd have to score and analyze more than six hundred sets of tests just to get to that starting point. It was amazing to see a group of teachers willingly agree to take on such a huge project.

We had high hopes. We expected that

- by mid-November we'd be fighting on behalf of LD students in meetings of the school-based committee;
- by the end of January I'd be guiding classroom teachers to find creative ways to help the newly identified LD students within their regular classes;
- by spring we'd have between fifteen and twenty of our LD students officially diagnosed and placed; and,
- with that many pupils already identified, we'd probably be able to get a specialist assigned to the school for the following year.

It was going to be a rough road, but we knew we could do it.

In mid-October, before even the first test had been given, I was ordered to come to the school system's administrative offices for a meeting. I looked forward to the opportunity to share the news of our screening program. I expected all levels of the administration to be delighted.

The assistant superintendent in charge of special education sat at one end of a long conference table. Gathered around him were the school system's LD supervisor, another supervisor, another assistant superintendent, and two other LD consultants. Neither of the other two LD consultants had yet gotten any specific plans underway in her assigned school. I shared some of the highlights of what we had started at Washington.

I never had the chance to give any details. The assistant superintendent in charge of special education furrowed his eyebrows and glowered at me. "Lady, what you're doing is 'identifying,' " he said. "And that's *against the law!*"

I nearly fell out of my chair. I believed that our screening program was both educationally sound and legal. I took the position that there was a difference between screening and identifying, but nothing I said made any impression on the big boss at all. The others may not have agreed with him, but no one spoke up against him.

Totally unprepared for the assistant superintendent's reaction, and with no one giving any support to my position, I listened in astonishment as our program was torn to shreds. We were *ordered* to abandon our screening.

Most teachers give up their fight for an LD child long before they get to an assistant superintendent. Most teachers have been around long enough to know you can't beat "the system."

Most teachers truly do care. They fail to get help for LD children for three basic reasons: (1) They are not trained to recognize learning disabilities. (2) They don't have the time or energy to devote to the needs of just one child. (3) They know that to help one particular child they will have to wade hip-deep into red tape and might have to take on the whole system.

## It Takes an Act of Congress to Get Help for an LD Child

In reading the dismal stories told in this chapter, one wonders that any of the learning-disabled are ever helped. It is obvious that parents cannot rely on the schools to identify these children and provide them with the special instruction they must have in order to learn. But the federal government has recently given parents a powerful weapon in demanding that their learning-disabled children get the help they need.

Public Law 94–142 was passed by Congress in 1977 and went into full effect in September, 1978. This law clearly states that public schools *must* meet *all* the educational needs of *all* their pupils free of cost. The blind, the deaf, the mentally retarded, the emotionally disturbed, the learning-disabled—for exceptional children as well as "normal" ones, a free and appropriate education *must* be provided under the law.

As might be expected, PL 94–142 includes many complex procedures and guidelines. These make testing and placement a slow and complicated process. However, the guidelines protect children from being shoved into programs in which they don't really belong.

Public Law 94–142 makes it possible for parents to go to their child's school and request, or even demand, testing. It makes it possible for parents to insist on appropriate instruction and therapy for a child who has already been diagnosed as learning-disabled. It makes it possible to get somebody to listen.

The law is still new. School systems are still fumbling around for ways to live with it and make it work. It's going to place a heavy burden on school budgets. It's going to put a huge strain on the already overworked school psychologists and special education teachers of all types.

And schools are going to find ways around the law. Even during the first year that PL 94–142 was in effect, many public schools found loopholes. They could no longer refuse to test a child, and once a child had been diagnosed as needing special help, they could no longer refuse him that help. But—if the forms hadn't been filled out properly, if there wasn't a huge mass of convincing evidence, if any small part of the identification procedure had not been followed exactly—the placement committee could refuse to consider the case. Unfortunately, it was all perfectly legal. LD children are not necessarily going to get the proper type of education simply because a law has been passed.

It's also possible that PL 94–142 might even do more harm than good. Schools might merely pour more and more students into already existing LD classes. That would allow the school systems to keep within the letter of the law. They could claim that they were providing appropriate instruction simply because all learning-disabled children were in classes taught by LD teachers.

Four conditions are required for a class to be appropriate for learning-disabled students. A class must have (1) a specially trained teacher, (2) special methods of instruction, (3) special books and materials, and (4) a small number of students— ideally, between six and ten. Many school systems pretend that the methods, materials, and class size are not important. They are wrong. If *any* of the four factors is missing, an appropriate class for LD students is *not* being provided—and the law is being violated.

## A Degree Does Not an Expert Make

There are so many out-and-out quacks in the field of learning disabilities that parents and teachers don't know whom to believe. And among experts who *do* know what they're talking about, there are so many vastly different approaches and theories that the specialists don't believe each other. They don't even agree among themselves as to what a learning disability is! It has gotten to the point that you just don't know who can be trusted. A string of degrees is no guarantee.

There is a state superintendent of special education who has a Ph.D. in psychology. He is said to be an expert in testing and diagnosis. He's in charge of all the LD programs in his entire state. Yet he has never taught a single LD child! How can this man guide LD teachers if he has never personally taught disabled children?

A young woman had a shiny new master's degree in learning disabilities from an excellent Southern university. She knew how to read a set of test scores (though she was not qualified to do the testing herself) and prescribe therapy for disabled children.

But she had never taught an LD child. She had many ideas, but had never tried out a single one of them.

This girl was unusual. She had sense enough to realize that her degree was not enough. She was not yet qualified to start work in her field.

The last time I saw her, she was looking for someone to supervise her as she learned to teach real LD children.

As I stood by the potato salad at a Cub Scout picnic, a mother proudly told me, "My son was diagnosed as learning-disabled at the age of three." It turned out that their pediatrician was a self-proclaimed expert on learning disabilities. He prided himself on recognizing all his little LD patients long before they reached school age.

She felt that this doctor had positively saved her son from certain doom.

I hope her pediatrician was the miracle worker she believed him to be, and not the quack I suspected.

Every LD expert has his own pet theory about treatment. Diets, color-coded alphabets, exercises, eye glasses, perceptual/motor training, eye-movement patterning, medication—a huge variety of possible cures have been proposed. A tremendous amount of research is being done. And a lot of it looks very promising. There's no question about it—someday someone will find *the cure*. But to the best of my knowledge, it has not been found yet.

## Hope for the Future

Learning disabilities is a new field in education. In the past, those with the necessary training could get a teacher's certificate in such special areas as physical handicaps, mental retardation, education of the deaf, etc. Then, in the mid-1970s, states began adding learning disabilities to the list of teaching fields they would recognize as areas of special education.

Once states began to certify teachers in the field of learning disabilities, colleges all over the country scrambled to put together programs. They were eager to offer training that would allow their graduates to qualify for positions in this new field. Well-trained experts were needed to direct and teach in these new programs. But experts were very scarce. In their haste, many colleges threw together shoddy programs. Thus, in the late 1970s, we are seeing many poorly trained specialists who were products of these makeshift programs. It is not at all uncommon to find certified LD teachers who don't know how to read a set of test scores or guide a classroom teacher in working with an LD child. Many have had no experience in actually teaching LD children. Many with a master's degree or Ph.D. have been taught a dab of this and a dab of that (often termed the "eclectic approach") but have no deep understanding of any one systematic method of LD therapy.

Public Law 94–142, new college training programs, and the certification of teachers in new areas have created a great demand for specialists in learning disabilities. Right now, many LD specialists with just a bachelor's degree are better trained than those with a Ph.D. As universities and colleges refine and improve their programs, more and more LD specialists will be highly qualified in their field.

The improved training of LD teachers can certainly be expected to carry over to the training of regular classroom teachers as well. There is a chance that by the year 2000 every school will have an LD specialist and every teacher will know how to recognize and work with LD children.

# WHAT TO DO WHEN PROFESSIONAL HELP IS NOT AVAILABLE:
## Adaptive Techniques

IN SPITE OF THE NEW LAWS, THERE WILL CONtinue to be LD children who do not get the help they need.

The bright child's high intelligence helps him to compensate for his learning disability. Such a child rarely qualifies for admission to public school LD programs because he seldom falls two years below grade level. Most public school programs are limited to those who are two or more years behind. Small private and church-related schools may never be able to afford special services for their LD students. Children with less common learning disabilities will probably continue to be ignored; they don't fit into programs aimed at teaching those with the more common types of specific language disabilities that center on problems with reading. And, as always, some LD children either will not be recognized at all or will be turned down by placement committees. No matter what the reasons, there will always be LD children who cannot get professional help. In such cases, parents and regular classroom teachers need some guidance. (In fact, all parents of LD children need this type of guidance. Those whose youngsters are getting professional help should look to their child's therapist as a source of advice. Part of good LD therapy includes counseling parents.)

## Get an Official Diagnosis

No matter how remote the area or how poor the school system, psychologists are available to test children at no cost to the parents. Even though the interpretation of the test results may be incorrect (and many of them are), the testing will provide one key piece of information. Through use of either the Stanford-Binet Intelligence Scale or the Wechsler Intelligence Scale for Children—Revised, the psychologist can get a reliable IQ score. (See Chapter 7 for further explanation concerning the meaning of such scores.)

In addition to the testing available through the local schools, most counties have some type of public clinic where a psychological evaluation can be obtained at very low cost. Most such clinics have well-trained psychologists who are experienced in testing children, although they often know very little about learning disabilities. While specialists at local clinics often cannot tell you if a child is learning-disabled, they *can* tell you if he is either mentally retarded or emotionally disturbed. So the information they provide is usually quite valuable.

Many colleges, universities, and hospitals have clinics that specialize in learning disabilities. Sometimes getting a child tested at one of these clinics is very expensive, but not always. Through the family doctor or pediatrician, the public school psychologist or social worker, local mental health agencies, or the National Association for Children with Learning Disabilities, parents can be guided in their search for such clinics in their area.

In seeking a good diagnosis, it is important to remember that many people will want to help the child, but most won't know how.

## Do Not Try to Teach Your Own Child

In order to help a child, his teacher must be calm, patient, confident, and understanding. Many adults are capable of maintaining this attitude with someone else's child; very few can be this unemotional with their own children. Doctors do not treat members of their own families. Parents should not teach their own children.

Yes, the LD child needs therapy. He also needs parents. Of the two, he needs parents more.

Parents should not ruin their role as parents by trying to be teachers as well. Rather, they should love, care, try to understand, sympathize, and help the child adapt. The LD child, more than most children, needs a home with fun and laughter and kite flying and fishing trips and picnics in the park. He needs to be helped to find activities outside of school that will give him success and pleasure. More than he needs anything else, the LD child needs a place where he can feel good about himself whether he reads well or not.

Anyone who is around an LD child can help him feel accepted and loved just as he is—but parents can do this best.

## Assume Responsibility

When professional LD therapy is not available, the parents of a learning-disabled child must be *totally* responsible for two things: (1) They must see to it that their child does not become emotionally damaged. (2) They must see to it that their child gets an education despite his learning disability. Even when therapy is available, these responsibilities still belong to the parents.

## Prevent Emotional Damage

In leading an LD child to an honest acceptance and understanding of his own disability, parents must be sure that they never do or say anything to make him feel guilty or ashamed of something for which he is not to blame. The youngster's home should be the one place in the world where he can count on finding understanding and encouragement. Unless parents work toward this goal, the child will develop strong feelings of guilt and worthlessness.

A very attractive and intelligent LD student of mine was not diagnosed until he was twenty-two. Bob stayed in high school until he was twenty-one, but his disability was so severe that he could not pass enough courses to graduate. Never having met a single person who understood his problem, he felt that he was a worthless failure and that it was all his own fault.

Bob loved to travel. He had hitchhiked all over the country. But he had never stayed in any one place for more than just a few days. He once told me, "I was afraid that if I stayed long enough for people to get to know me, they wouldn't like me."

Bob was a very gentle, loving person. Yet he had been a loner for years. It wasn't that he didn't like people. He was afraid to let anybody get close to him. He was afraid of being rejected. He believed that anyone who found out about his poor spelling and reading would think he was a worthless bum—the same way he saw himself.

In order to accept and like himself, Bob had to learn to understand his own learning disability. After he recognized some of the beauty in himself, he opened up to let others see it, too.

Convincing an LD child that he is not stupid is always a long process. It cannot be accomplished by one speech that is never repeated. Day by day things will happen to make him feel dumb: he'll spend three hours studying for a test, then flunk it flat; he'll misread *ask* as *ass* right in front of his whole class; he'll get thrown out of art class because he's so clumsy with a ruler and scissors that the teacher thinks he's not even trying; he'll be suspended from high school because he ripped up his Shakespeare book and threw it at his English teacher's feet. As such situations arise, the child will need help getting over the hurt feelings, anger, and embarrassment. He will often need to have someone calmly lead him to figure out which of his LD symptoms caused the problem, how that particular problem is different from general stupidity, and how to avoid letting the problem get him into another bad situation in the future.

A student teacher was giving dictation to my LD class of ten- to twelve-year-olds. She was reading sentences which the students were writing on their papers. I was observing.

Sam, an older boy with a very quick temper and a severe disability, was having trouble keeping up. Wanting Miss Long to slow down, he raised his hand once to get her attention. But she didn't notice. Struggling with his spelling and his handwriting, he tried to catch up. Finally he slammed his pencil down on his desk, folded his arms across his chest with a "hummpph," and gave up. The color rose in his neck and face as he glared straight ahead to fight back the tears. Sam was very near exploding.

Still Miss Long didn't notice.

Several of the boys glanced at him with sympathy. They understood his frustration and would have offered help if they could. But they had problems enough of their own—the dictation was still going on.

There were only five more minutes until break. I decided that as long as Sam didn't explode, I would not interfere. Those five minutes seemed to last for hours.

Finally Miss Long collected the papers. When she took Sam's from his desk, she commented, "You've only got the first part. Why didn't you finish?"

"I didn't *want* to," he snarled.

Miss Long didn't push it. She dismissed the boys for break.

I caught Sam's attention and motioned toward the door. "I'd like to speak to you in private."

In heavy silence, he followed me out into the hall.

The rest of my students moved freely around us on their way to the drinking fountain and bathroom. But they totally ignored us. (The area just outside our door was recognized as the place where my pupils could talk with me in private despite the hordes of children streaming by.)

I put an arm around Sam's shoulder. He stared at the floor. I tried not to be too gentle—that would have made him cry, and embarrassed him further. "I want to compliment you for the way you handled that situation," I began.

He didn't answer by even a nod.

I went on, "Miss Long didn't notice that you got stuck—and I'll speak to her about that. For your part, you handled your anger well. You didn't throw anything or shout anything nasty. . . ." I paused to let him think about how much his behavior had improved over the past six months. "Your learning disability makes spelling really tough. For you, and some of the other guys too, these dictations are really murder."

Sam nodded his head in agreement. He was winning his battle over the welling tears, but still didn't dare look at me.

"You *were* rude to Miss Long. But considering how upset you were, what you said was not all that bad." I gave his shoulder a squeeze, then concluded, "You go on in the bathroom and get yourself a drink, walk around the building for a few minutes, and cool off."

Sam was pretty well back together. I gave him a pat on the rear and he ambled off down the hall.

When I explained the situation to Miss Long, she was surprised and ashamed. "But why didn't he raise his hand?" she asked.

"He did raise his hand—once. But you were dictating and didn't notice."

She shook her head. Now my intern was on the verge of tears.

I tried to calm her down while also making her understand. "I know you don't have eyes in the back of your head. When a kid puts his hand up one time for three seconds, you won't always notice. That's not where you blew it."

Miss Long stared at me.

As gently as I could, I laid it on the line. "A 'normal' kid will flap his hand around in the air all day and insist that you wait while he catches up. But Sam's LD. He hates dictations. For him, they're hard. He's ashamed of just how hard—and besides, if there were any possible way around it, he'd rather not do them at all. If getting hit in the head with a two-by-four would get him out of doing a dictation, he'd take the two-by-four.

A small smile fluttered at the corners of Miss Long's mouth. She was beginning to get the idea.

"It's a wonder he gave you a chance by raising his hand even once—but he did. And you missed it. Okay, so now what do you do?"

"Yeah, really." Miss Long nodded. "What do I do?"

"First of all, you get to know your kids. No matter what you're doing, you need to know in advance which ones are going to have trouble with it. Dictations are tough. They all hate them. But four or five of the guys have a *special* hate for dictation."

"Sam, and Bobby, and Ted . . ." she named a few, paused, then added two more.

"Right." She had selected the same ones I would have picked. "So during dictation, you keep a sharp eye on those five. Don't let them bog down. Don't let them get lost. Don't wait for them to get into trouble or fall apart. Cruise that room. Watch those papers. Tune in to those pencils. You can't teach LD kids standing up in front of the room like a post. Move around. Watch. Get close."

We discussed it together for a few minutes; then Miss Long asked, "What do I do about Sam? Do you think I should apologize?"

I advised, "An apology would be nice, if it's genuine. It would help him to know that teachers make mistakes, too. But the main thing is for you and Sam to work out a way so it won't happen again. Help him see that it's his learning disability that makes dictations so hard for him. Then find a way where you and he can *both* take some responsibility for his keeping up in the future."

She nodded and started back into the room.

I tapped her on the shoulder. "Then, take him in the back of the room and give him the dictation."

Miss Long seemed stunned. She didn't complain, but her face plainly showed that she thought I was being too tough a task-master on Sam.

"It's like the law of gravity," I explained. "No matter what happens, the students get their work done. *Nothing*—bad behavior, tantrums, misunderstandings, apple polishing—*nothing* can get one of these kids out of doing his work."

"Right." She smiled with real understanding.

Miss Long took Sam to a table at the back of the room. They talked comfortably together for quite a while, then did the dictation. They both had learned something important about themselves.

In the above incident, Sam was helped to understand his own learning disability. He was also helped to deal with his anger.

Learning-disabled children feel a lot of anger. They must be taught to deal with it.

Many adults make the terrible mistake of denying the LD child his right to feel angry. He's got a problem. He's got a problem that embarrasses him, makes him look stupid, and prevents him from doing many of the things he wants to do. He does not *want* to be learning-disabled. But he *is*—and he hates it.

Of course he gets angry.

The anger itself is not bad. It's what he does with his anger that causes trouble and frightens others.

When an LD child (or any other child, for that matter) is already furious about something, it is wrong to tell him that he should not feel angry. He *is* angry. He needs someone to help him figure out what to *do* with his anger. He needs to get rid of it.

The way to get rid of anger is to express it. And, of course, the best way to express it is in some way that does no harm. This is something children must be taught.

There are two ways to express anger that seem to work best: physical and vocal. (A psychologist could perhaps explain why that is so; I merely know from experience that it is true.) An angry child needs to release a burst of energy by ripping, throwing, smashing, jumping up and down, kicking, running, crushing, pounding, stomping, hitting, squeezing—or by screaming, yelling, shrieking, cursing, bellowing, shouting, swearing. One or the other or both, directed at something that will not be damaged and won't fight back, will use up all the anger.

My boys were always getting into fist fights during their touch football games. If a play didn't work out right, one of them would get angry and throw the ball at somebody—hard. A fight was almost always the result.

We solved the problem by agreeing that anger does make a person want to throw something. That method of releasing anger would be allowed provided two rules were observed: nothing would be thrown at another person; and the one who hurled the ball halfway across the field would be the one to go and get it.

Throwing the ball didn't appeal to everybody, though. Some of my students were more prone to shouting and cursing at someone when they got angry. A few simple swear words almost always led to real filth, followed by references to "your mama . . . ." And then the fur would fly.

We solved this problem by agreeing that anger does make a person want to scream. Anyone overwhelmed by this need would be allowed to go over by the woods and shout anything he felt like shouting. Anything the rest of us overheard was ignored. As soon as the anger had been spent, the screamer was taken back into the game with no questions or comments. (The screaming never lasted more than three minutes.)

Those rules saved the guys from a lot of fights.

Fifth-graders Ted, Bobby, and Ken hated math. Though their

problems were different, all were struggling to learn second-grade arithmetic. I would work with them closely, then leave them to work alone for five or ten minutes. It never failed—each of them would ask permission to go to the bathroom during that time when they were supposed to work a row or two of problems on their own.

One day one of them slipped and asked, "May I go in the bathroom and punch the can?"

These three had discovered that when they got upset over their math, they could get rid of their anger by punching and banging on the trash can in the boys' bathroom. They would work as long as they could stand it, take out their fury on the beat-up old trash barrel, and return to finish their math. (We got permission from a very understanding principal to use the trash can as our official punching bag.)

Sometimes Bobby would shuffle over to me from some game or work assignment, muttering through clenched teeth, "I'm about to explode. Can I go kick the fence?"

No matter where or when, as long as he planned to come back and face the situation again, my answer was always something like, "You sure may. You may shout some, too, if you want. . . ."

"I'll be back in a minute," he'd say, and stomp off to have his private, harmless tantrum. Every time, within two minutes Bobby would be back at work or play as though nothing had happened. But something important had occurred in those two minutes: he had gotten rid of his anger.

In most cases, the parents of a learning-disabled child cannot control the way he is treated by other people. The child will often need to be defended from friends, relatives, neighbors, and playmates who do not understand his disability. Despite the best efforts to protect him, however, there will be many times when he is hurt or embarrassed by his learning problem and the way outsiders react to it.

But within the home, such pain and embarrassment should not be permitted. Brothers and sisters are going to disagree and fight. Parents, however, must see to it that their children fight fair. The LD child's disability must never be allowed to become a special target for insults.

Below are five situations that are typical of the problems that arise between all brothers and sisters. With each are two statements that an angry child might direct toward his LD brother. One is an example of what parents must not allow; the other would be fair in an argument.

**Situation:** The LD child wants to borrow his older brother's bicycle.
**Foul:** "No, you can't borrow my bicycle. I wouldn't trust anyone as dumb as you with *my* new bike!"
**Fair:** "No, you can't use my bike. The last time you took it you left it in the park!"

**Situation:** The LD child and his older sister disagree on whose turn it is to do the dishes.
**Foul:** "I do the dishes on Monday, Wednesday, and Friday. Today is Thursday. You can't even tell the days of the week, you klutz!"
**Fair:** "I remember I did the dishes last night because we had spaghetti and *I* had to clean that yukky pot. Tonight's your turn and you're not going to get out of it."

**Situation:** The LD child and his brother who shares a room with him are arguing over cleaning up.
**Foul:** "All of this mess in here is yours. Your homework papers, your schoolwork—you make a mess out of everything you touch!"
**Fair:** "I refuse to clean up this mess. It's all yours. All this junk scattered all over the floor is yours—not mine.

**Situation:** The LD child spills milk at the dinner table.

**Foul:** "Can't you do anything right? Go get a rag and clean that up."

**Fair:** "Look at the mess. Go get a rag and clean it up."

**Situation:** The second-grade sister shows an A+ spelling paper to her sixth-grade LD brother.

**Foul:** "I got an A+ on *my* spelling. Take a good look at it. Looking at *my* papers is the only way *you'll* ever see A+'s!"

**Fair:** "I got an A+ on my spelling paper. I'm the best speller in my class."

(Sometimes the tone of voice is as telling as the words used. In the situation just above, the fair statement would become foul if it sounded like this: "*I* got an A+ on *my* spelling paper. *I'm* the *best* speller in *my* class.")

The four ways in which parents must guard against emotional damage to their LD child bear repeating. No matter what the school is or is not doing to help the child, it is the responsibility of the *parents* (1) to help him understand that his learning disability is not his fault and that it is no cause for guilt or shame; (2) to teach him that he is learning-disabled and *not* stupid; (3) to teach him to deal with his anger; and (4) to protect him from his brothers and sisters so that his home can be a place where he feels loved and accepted no matter what is going on in school.

### Educate Him Despite His Learning Disability

Many LD children never acquire the information needed for successful living. It isn't that they can't learn and understand the facts of history, science, health, and other subjects—it's that they're not able to read and write about them. The LD child is limited in how he learns; parents need to see to it that he is not also limited in what he learns.

Parents seem to think it's cheating if someone reads their child's social studies or science book to him. If he has an assignment for reading class—yes, he should read it himself. If he has an assignment for a science class, *who* reads it is unimportant. He's not being taught to read about science; he's being taught the ideas and information of science.

My first LD student was a boy I worked with while I was still in high school. Jack was a very bright ninth-grader who was a total nonreader.

With the school's permission, Jack's parents paid me to come to their house every night and act as their son's secretary. I read him all his assignments, asked him the required questions, and recorded his answers. If he had to write a report, I read the material to him, then he dictated his report to me.

In school Jack was treated as though he were blind. He was never asked to read or write. He *was* expected to participate actively in all other class activities and to learn the material being taught. His tests were given to him orally, but were exactly the same as the ones his classmates did in writing.

Jack was a good student and made good grades. He learned everything taught in his junior high school courses despite the fact that he could neither read nor write.

At that time and place, no one was able to teach Jack to read. Yet his parents made sure he got as much as he could out of the education offered him in their local public schools. When Jack graduated from high school, he was "illiterate" but not "uneducated." And there is a huge difference.

Parents must see to it that their child learns in spite of his learning disability.

## ADJUSTMENTS IN THE HOME

It is amazing how many parents allow life at home to be ruined by an LD child. The process starts out slowly and gradually builds. As a first-grader, the youngster is helped with his reading homework for perhaps half an hour a night. In the second grade, the child requires an hour or so of help with reading, spelling, and math. When he gets to the fourth or fifth grade, his parents are spending almost four hours a day hunched over school books at the kitchen table. The pattern is always deadly.

The LD child hates it. He has no self-confidence and can't learn anything by himself. He's learned to depend on those at home to teach him. Instead of fighting his books for hours, he wants to play and watch TV like other children his age. He hates the entire mess, but doesn't know how to change it. His whole day, his whole life, centers around his learning disability. He becomes very hard to get along with as his unhappiness grows. More and more of his time is spent screaming and fighting in rage, or crying and sobbing with hurt feelings and shame.

Brothers and sisters hate it. Their home has been turned into a study hall to help this one brother. It doesn't seem fair. The LD child gets all the parents' attention. He's always busy doing his schoolwork, so he gets out of doing household chores. His brothers and sisters think he's a spoiled brat who gets away with murder. They are jealous of all the special care he gets. They resent the way his problem deprives them of a normal, happy home life. They take these feelings out on the LD child and their parents. They tease and pick on their LD brother. They complain and gripe and fume at their parents. In their anger and frustration, they too become hard to get along with. The brothers and sisters don't have the power to straighten out their messed-up home life. But they do have the power to make the situation worse—much worse. And that's what they usually do.

The parents hate the situation, too. After a hard day at work, they'd like to spend a quiet evening relaxing in front of the

TV, or a pleasant few hours at the bowling alley. They can't hire a baby-sitter and go out for dinner and a movie. They can't leave the children and go next door for a visit with a neighbor. If they did, who would help the LD child with his homework?

The parents feel trapped. They believe that it is their duty to spend night after night working with their learning-disabled child. "With both of us helping him, it takes at least three hours a night for him to get his homework done," they tell their friends. That one child has become their purpose in life. In making sacrifices for him, they believe they are doing what is right.

Their motive has become fear. They are afraid their child will fail in school if they don't help him and that he will blame them for his failure. They are afraid he will grow to hate them. They are afraid he will give up and drop out, or run away, or turn to drugs, or have a nervous breakdown.

Fear and anger and guilt keep the parents going. They are angry that the LD child won't cooperate and doesn't even seem to try. They are angry that they have to give up so much for this one child; angry that their other children make the situation worse; angry that fate would give them such a child in the first place. Their anger turns to guilt, which is then added to the guilt they already feel for having brought such a child into the world.

The vicious circle continues because the parents are afraid that, if they broke it, something might happen to make them feel even more guilty.

Instead of one suffering LD child, we now have a whole miserable, suffering family. Everybody is angry; everybody feels guilty; everybody is afraid. The parents quarrel and argue with each other and with all their children. The children argue and fight among themselves. The normal pleasures found in a home cannot exist in such an atmosphere.

The problem is not the LD child, and it is not his disability. The problem is the way the parents are handling the disability when the child is at home. There is a better way.

### Avoiding the Trap: Rules for Parents

1. As much as possible, avoid sitting down to work *with* the LD child.

Set up his study place in his room or some other quiet part of the house where he will not be disturbed. If he needs help with a question or a difficult word, let him come to someone to get assistance, then return to his room to work alone.

For the more severely disabled child, set up his study place where he can ask for help without leaving his desk or making someone come to him. Working at the kitchen table while his mother is fixing dinner allows the child to get help when he needs it but still allows him to work alone as much as he can. He can be close to those who can assist him *without* keeping them from their own activities.

When it is necessary to sit down to help the child with his work, set exact limits before you start. For example: "You have ten pages to read. Okay, I'll read the first three pages to you, then you read the rest aloud to me while I peel the potatoes." Or, "You have to write a book report? You get it all planned and written down, and I'll give you half an hour right after dinner to help you correct your spelling." Or, "We'll read your social studies book together for twenty minutes tonight at bedtime." Stick to the limits you set. If the child has a fit when you have done what was promised—too bad. Leave the room and go about your business.

2. Set time limits on homework.

No young child (in the first or second grade) should ever spend more than an hour a day on homework. By himself, with some help, or with a lot of assistance—any child less than eight years old who has really worked for one hour should be told to quit whether he has finished or not. (If he is unable to finish his work in the one-hour limit, the matter should be taken up with his teacher.)

Older children need time limits, too. The limits below provide a good rule of thumb:

third- through sixth-graders—1½ to two hours
seventh- through ninth-graders—two to three hours
tenth- through twelfth-graders—three to four hours

It should be kept in mind that these limits apply to time actually spent working. Time off for daydreaming, tantrums, trips to the refrigerator, etc., do *not* count. It is hoped that no student will study his full limit every night. These are to be thought of as cutoff points for doing regular homework assignments. If the student can't get his work done in the time allowed by these limits, something is wrong. (Special projects, term papers, reports, and studying for exams might sometimes require extra time. Usually they should not.)

These time limits are for the *child*. The parents should not spend nearly this much time working with him.

3. Limit the amount of time that will be given to helping the child with his homework.

As a general rule, parents should make themselves available to assist their LD child with no more than half his homework.

A third-grader with a disability in reading and spelling could do an arithmetic worksheet alone. (This would probably take about fifteen or twenty minutes.) Someone could then give him forty-five minutes of help: fifteen minutes to read his social studies with him; thirty minutes to help him find some information he needs for a special science project. His remaining time would be spent working alone on the project. (Notice that no-body checks over his arithmetic.)

A sixth-grader with a writing disability could read his social studies and prepare the answers to the chapter questions by him-self. Someone could then give him forty-five minutes to help him write out his answers to the questions. If there was time left over, this person could copy half of his math problems out of the book for him. The student would then use the rest of his two-hour limit to finish his math alone.

No matter how old the child is or how much homework he has, parents should seldom devote more than 1½ hours a night to helping him with his studies. Severely disabled high school and college students sometimes need more help than this al-lows. In such cases the parents should make arrangements for their child to get the help he needs outside the home. (See rule 5 below.)

Make sure the child knows exactly how much help he can count on, from whom it will come, and when it will be avail-able. This will encourage him to use his helper wisely. He will know that when the time is up, his assistant will quit and leave him to finish his work on his own.

It is usually best to get the child to do his part of the home-work first. Save the assistance until he has done as much as he can on his own. By doing this, you avoid having the child say, "If you won't stay here and help me, then I won't do it." Do not put him in the position where he can punish you for not helping. Try to make him feel that he is given some help as a reward for doing the best he can on his own.

4. Limit the type of help that will be given.

Be sure the child needs the help he is given. Parents often continue to assist a child with a subject he finds difficult even though he has reached the point where he can do it alone. Helping him has just become a habit.

A child who needed help with his math in the fourth grade will not necessarily need such help in the eighth grade. Give him a chance to succeed on his own. He can outgrow his need for help only if his parents will let him.

If a child is capable of reading and understanding his social studies by himself, let him take the hour he needs to do it rather than pitching in so he can get it done faster. If it's a day when he has a lot of homework and is pressed for time—yes, he needs help. But do not let meeting that occasional need become a habit.

If a child with a math disability needs help working the problems, let him copy them from the book himself. If a child with a writing disability needs help writing his math problems, let him work them himself. A child who cannot read at all needs someone to read *to* him; a child who can read to some extent needs someone to read *with* him. Offer assistance only with those things that the child cannot do by himself.

Be sure the child gets a "secretary" for a helper, not a teacher. Secretaries do the reading and writing, not the teaching or thinking. If the student does not completely understand the material being read, that is not the helper's problem. If he gives an incorrect answer to a study question, it is not up to his helper to change it. The other students in the child's class read the assignment and answer the questions by themselves. Almost all of them will get at least a few of their answers wrong. The LD child may not be able to read and write his work all by himself. But he must be allowed to do his own thinking—which is to say, he must be given the chance to make his own mistakes.

5. The helper does not have to be one of the child's parents.

In choosing the best possible person to assist the child with his homework, three qualifications must be considered:

a. Most important, the helper must be able to work peacefully with the child. Sarcasm, harsh criticism, arguing, sulking, tears, or shouting mean that the wrong person has been chosen.

b. College degrees or high school diplomas are not necessary. The helper does not have to be terrific at reading, writing, spelling, or the other skills the child may be studying. He merely needs to be more skillful than the child. An average student in junior high school could easily help a second- or third-grader.

c. The assistant should be a volunteer. Anyone forced into the job is likely to have the wrong attitude. An aunt, an uncle, a special neighbor or friend—almost anyone could prove to be the ideal person. (Caution: Never insist that an older brother or sister take on the job. If one of them wants to pitch in—great. If not, look elsewhere. Other children in the family do not owe their LD brother this kind of help.)

Finding a person who works well with the child is the trick!

Parents tend to feel guilty if they don't help the child themselves. They don't seem to realize that parents and their child can seldom work peacefully together on the child's homework. There are also many parents who simply do not have the time, energy, or patience to become directly involved with their youngster's studies. Most LD children definitely need some kind of assistance with their homework. It *is* the responsibility of parents to see that they get it. But there is no reason that this help must come from a parent, family member, neighbor, or friend. Often the best solution involves finding someone totally outside the home. An older child who needs more than 1½ hours of help a day *should* get this assistance elsewhere.

Professional therapy and tutoring are usually very expensive. But getting someone to help an LD child with his homework does not necessarily have to cost anything. Churches, community centers, civic associations, clubs and fraternities on college campuses, service groups—many organizations are looking for opportunities to volunteer the time and energy of their members for helping others.

One of my boys had a young college student assigned to him through the program called Big Brothers. As the two became friends, the "big brother" saw that my LD student had some very special needs. They spent many happy evenings together working on homework. After the two had been together for a year, the college student got his "little brother" into a special summer program at a private LD clinic.

As part of a church project, a family in my neighborhood "adopted" a widower who lived in a local home for the elderly. They wanted to share some of the joys of their family life with a lonely older person. The man they befriended took a special liking to one of their sons, who was learning-disabled. He found it a great pleasure to help the child with his homework. The boy and the old man were soon working together regularly. Not only did the homework get done, but both were experiencing the joy of a loving and caring relationship.

## ADJUSTMENTS IN THE SCHOOL

The parents of a learning-disabled child must keep in close touch with their child's teacher. Through good communication, many of the horrible things that happen to LD children can be avoided. Parents should make the first move in establishing communication. That can easily be done by having a conference with the teacher in early September.

Everybody assumes that the teacher knows all about her new class when school opens in the fall. After all, she has files full of records.

Don't believe it!

It is true that schools keep a permanent folder on each of their students. But half the time the child's file can't be found—or is full of stuff that gives no hint of a learning disability—or is simply never seen. Worse still, test scores and psychologists' reports on LD children are often locked away in a "confidential" file somewhere down in the basement. These confidential reports are sometimes kept so secret that even the child's teacher never gets to see them.

If your child is learning-disabled, do not assume that the teacher already knows it. Make an appointment at the very beginning of the school year and go in and *tell* her. You can and should assume that she cares and wants to do everything in her power to help. But do not assume that she already knows.

In that first conference, parents need to share the important knowledge they have about their LD child. (*Parents* means mother *and* father if at all possible.) Once the teacher knows the purpose of the visit, she can be expected to ask many questions. She will probably want to know about the child's past performance in school, his homelife, his particular strengths and weaknesses, his interests and hobbies, and so on. Learning all she can about him will make life easier for her and the child. Parents will usually find their child's teacher interested and cooperative.

During this first conference, the subject of homework, including how the child's assignments must be adjusted, should be discussed thoroughly. The teacher needs to know what kind of help the child will get at home. She needs to understand the parents' rules about limits on how long the child may work and how much help he may have. Once she knows what assistance she can count on from the home, she will be able to adjust and adapt accordingly.

The most important object of this first conference is to establish communication. The parents want the teacher to know that they will work with her. They want her to feel free to call them any time there is a question or problem.

They want her to know what she can expect from them.

But it will be too soon then to tell her what they expect from her. Suggestions of things that have worked well in the past, some questions about how the teacher will be running her class, and talk of possible adjustments that might be needed are appropriate. However, parents should not ask for, or expect to be given, a detailed plan of how the teacher intends to work with their LD child. In early September the teacher cannot yet know the child well enough to make firm commitments about her methods of teaching him. At this point it is very important for parents simply to expect the best from the teacher and to indicate to her a willingness to be reasonable and cooperative.

It takes at least a month for a good teacher to develop an adequate understanding of a child's needs and abilities. During that time she establishes a relationship with the child and decides how she can best work with him. The parents will sometimes be allowed to take part in the process. Many teachers like to communicate with parents through regular notes or phone calls during that first crucial month. Others prefer not to be influenced during that period. In either case, the parents should make an appointment for a second conference before they conclude the first one. A strategy meeting should be scheduled for early in October. Before they leave the first conference, the parents should also get the teacher's home phone number so they can reach her in case a serious problem arises in the meantime.

By the first of October the teacher can be expected to be ready to make definite commitments about how she will teach the child. Everyone needs to understand exactly what the teacher will and will not do on behalf of the LD child. That information is what the parents should gain from the second conference.

## Adjustments in Schoolwork

The object of adjusting the LD child's schoolwork is to increase his learning and decrease his frustration. Those goals could be accomplished in many ways that would be helpful to the child, but that would also be an impossible burden on the teacher. Just as parents are not going to spend three hours a night working with their child, a teacher can't be asked to spend three hours a night preparing special assignments for him.

However, there are many adjustments that the teacher can realistically be expected to make. The problem is that parents often don't know which possible solutions to the child's problem are workable and which are not. The guidelines below should help parents in making only reasonable requests of their child's teacher.

## Adjustments inside the Classroom

LD children need special consideration inside the classroom. Although the parents won't be directly involved in carrying out the required adjustments, it is their responsibility to see that they are made. Parents must be very careful that they expect only actions that are both necessary for their child and reasonably practical for the teacher. Basically, it is a matter of rights. The LD child has a right to be treated with the respect that a human being deserves. The teacher has a right to allocate her time in the way that she feels would be most beneficial to the entire class.

1. Expect: The child will not be criticized, shamed, scolded, or made to feel embarrassed or guilty about his learning disability. The teacher will not tell him he is lazy, stupid, stubborn, or worthless.

**Hope for:** The child will be encouraged to work around his learning problem while facing it honestly. The teacher will protect him from other children who tease or try to make him feel inferior.

**Don't ask:** In addition to helping the child deal effectively with his learning disability, the teacher will lead the entire class to be understanding of him and his special problems and needs.

2. **Expect:** The child will never be asked to do work he is totally incapable of doing.

**Hope for:** The child will be asked to do as much of the regular classwork as possible. When necessary, he will be given smaller amounts of the regular work, or special materials that teach him the same concepts at a level he can handle.

**Don't ask:** All the child's classwork will be adjusted to his needs and ability.

3. **Expect:** In reading, spelling, and math, the child will be given instruction appropriate to his level of skill. (No child reading at a second-grade level will be asked to work from a fifth-grade reading book, for example.)

**Hope for:** In the basic subject areas, the teacher will choose materials and make assignments in accordance with the child's level of skill *and* his individual strengths and weaknesses. (For instance, in describing a scene from a story, the rest of the children would be required to write a paragraph, while the LD child might be asked to draw an illustration.)

**Don't ask:** For reading, spelling, and math, the child will be placed in a very small group where the materials, assignments, and methods of instruction are carefully tailored to fit his level of skill, personal learning style, and needs.

4. **Expect:** The child will be a part of the regular program in such subjects as science, social studies, health, art, music, physical education, and drama, but will not be expected to read the books for himself.

**Hope for:** The teacher will help the child succeed within the regular school program in such subjects as science and social studies. She will encourage parents to read his home assignments with him or to him. Classwork will either be adjusted so that he can do it alone or a partner will be selected to assist him with reading and writing.

**Don't ask:** The regular programs in science, social studies, and other subjects will be taught in such a way that the child's learning disability will be no real handicap.

5. **Expect:** When both appropriate and possible, the teacher will allow the child to take tests aloud. She will either make arrangements to have someone read tests to him, or will allow the parents to provide that service by sending test materials home to them in a sealed envelope.

**Hope for:** When appropriate, the teacher will make the arrangements needed to allow the child to take tests orally.

**Don't ask:** All tests will be given orally, one-to-one, or in some other way that allows the child to show what he knows about the subject without having to read or spell.

**6. Expect:** The child will not be prevented from taking part in activities outside the classroom as punishment for poor performance in his school-work. Art, music, physical education, recess, or field trips will not be withheld from him on the ground that he did not get his work done or that he failed at some particular class assignment. Of course, those activities might be withheld as punishment for bad behavior.

**Hope for:** The child will be encouraged to take part in all activities outside the classroom. Movies, film strips, demonstrations, field trips, special projects, art, music, drama, physical education, etc., will be treated as worthwhile activities through which the child may find pleasure and success.

**Don't ask:** The teacher will help the child discover outlets in which he can find pleasure and success. The child will be guided in exploring various activities outside the regular classroom. His natural creativity will be prized, encouraged, and developed.

**7. Expect:** The child will not be allowed to become a bully. In demanding reasonable behavior, the teacher will not tolerate temper tantrums, lack of respect, rudeness, foul language, physical injury to other children, or damage to property.

**Hope for:** The child will not be allowed to develop behavior problems. The teacher will encourage him to express his anger and frustration in ways that do no harm to himself, to others, or to property.

**Don't ask:** The child will be taught to understand himself and his learning disability. In addition to being taught to deal with anger and frustration, he will be praised and rewarded for his real successes so that he will learn to find satisfaction in good behavior.

8. **Expect:** The teacher will cooperate with the parents.

**Hope for:** The teacher will take the lead in seeing that the school and the home are working together in the best interest of the child. She will make it a point to keep the parents informed about the child's progress, and will remain open to questions and suggestions.

**Don't ask:** The teacher will guide and coordinate the efforts of parents, psychologist, social worker, LD consultant, and others in their joint effort to help the child.

### Adjustments in Homework

Making it possible for an LD child to complete homework successfully requires *very* careful coordination between home and school. It is the parents' responsibility to see that there is a clear understanding between them and their child's teacher concerning types and sizes of assignments, time to be allowed, and help that will be provided. An attitude of trust and cooperation is essential. By establishing a mutually agreeable set of guidelines, most disasters can be avoided before they ever arise. Again, on the issue of homework, parents must be sure that what they ask of the teacher is both reasonable and practical.

1. **Expect:** The teacher will allow the parents to help the child with his regular homework.

   **Hope for:** By adjusting the work required of him in completing a class's homework assignment, the teacher will make it possible for the child to do much of his studying by himself. She will inform the parents about general subjects or particular assignments on which their help will be needed.

   **Don't ask:** The teacher will design all the child's homework so that he is capable of completing it by himself.

2. **Expect:** When an assignment cannot be completed within the time limit his parents allow, the child will not be penalized for failing to finish it.

   **Hope for:** The teacher will see to it that the child has no more homework than he can complete within the time his parents allow.

   **Don't ask:** The teacher will design special homework for the child that can be completed within the time his parents allow.

3. **Expect:** The teacher will allow one of her other students to see that the child has copied his homework assignment correctly from the blackboard.

**Hope for:** The teacher will personally check to see that the child has copied down his homework assignment correctly.

**Don't ask:** The teacher will write out homework assignments *for* the child.

4. **Expect:** The teacher will cheerfully explain a homework assignment to the parents if they can't figure it out and have to call her at home.

**Hope for:** The teacher will carefully explain homework assignments to the child and will encourage him to call her at home if he has trouble.

**Don't ask:** The teacher will see to it that the child understands every home assignment so completely that he never needs advice or help.

5. **Expect:** The teacher will accept work that the parents write for the child because he is not capable of writing it for himself, *provided* the child does the thinking and the work is in his own words.

**Hope for:** The teacher will help the child find ways to do his written homework for himself. She will let him answer questions with one or two words instead of whole sentences; she will accept one or two good sentences instead of a whole paragraph; she will accept a cassette tape recording in place of a long written report. Also, she will encourage him to express his ideas through projects and oral reports rather than through the usual written reports.

**Don't ask:** The child will not be assigned any written work that he cannot complete successfully by himself. He will be provided with worksheets on which questions are answered by filling in blanks or circling words. His math will be done in workbooks so the problems won't need to be copied. Answers to questions at the end of chapters in science, social studies, etc., will either be presented orally or will be recorded on a cassette tape and handed in. All written reports will be done *in* school under the direct supervision of the teacher. A casette tape recording can always be used to meet the requirements of any written home assignment.

**6. Expect:** Either the teacher will not count off for poor spelling outside of spelling class, *or* she will allow the parents to proofread and correct spelling errors for the child.

**Hope for:** In order to encourage the child to do as much of his own work as possible, the teacher will overlook poor spelling in all his written work outside of spelling class. When a word is such a jumble that the reader can't figure it out, the teacher will ask the child what was intended, then supply him with the correct spelling.

**Don't ask:** The child's work will be designed so that his poor spelling will not be a problem. When necessary, the teacher will help the child proofread his work for spelling errors.

## General Guidelines

In finding ways to adapt regular schoolwork so that the LD child can learn, three basic rules need to be remembered:

1. The home should not be turned into a classroom or study hall.

2. Adjustments should be made only in areas where the child is not capable of doing his work in the normal way.

3. The teacher should make some adjustments, too.

The object of these rules is simple but important: to help the learning-disabled child achieve more learning with less frustration.

# ·6·
# WHAT LD THERAPY CAN REALLY ACCOMPLISH:
## Do You Believe in Miracles?

THERAPY FOR LEARNING-DISABLED CHILDREN is a highly specialized kind of instruction. It is different from regular classroom teaching in four basic ways.

1. LD therapy is designed specifically to meet the special needs of a particular child. It is not a balanced program that attempts to teach all subjects and improve all skills. For example, a child with a writing disability might use his therapy session to work on eye/hand coordination, pencil control, handwriting, and copying. He would be taught to write sentences, paragraphs, stories, reports, and answers to questions. Drawing and making maps and charts might also be included. The writing and copying skills involved in math would probably be covered. The student would almost always spend his entire session with a pencil in his hand, working on his area of disability.

2. A program of LD therapy is based on a thorough diagnosis. A quick appraisal (see Chapter 2) does not give the type of precise information that a therapist needs in order to create a plan for teaching the student. Testing establishes the

nature and extent of the disability; then a program of therapy is designed.

3. LD therapy helps the child overcome basic problems that affect his ability to succeed in most areas of education.

> Lucinda was a lovely sixth-grade girl with a very puzzling disability. She had a good attitude, normal intelligence, and good skills in reading, writing, spelling, and math. No one was able to figure out how she could work so hard yet continue to fail so miserably.
>
> It was finally discovered that Lucinda had a problem with certain kinds of reasoning. She couldn't understand words that were broad enough to include different kinds of things. She didn't understand the relationship between cause and effect. She was unable to take a set of facts and draw a generalization from them.
>
> Her entire school program had to be adjusted. Every one of her teachers had to come up with special methods that would allow her to learn.
>
> Lucinda's LD therapy consisted of only one thing: teaching the girl to reason. Her therapist had to invent ways to do this. She would give the child a banana, an apple, and a pear and then ask, "What have you got?" She would show her a picture of a man all wrapped in bandages and then ask, "What happened?" She would take her outside under a tree and then ask, "What season is this?" After getting the correct answer, she'd ask, "Can you prove it?"
>
> Using everything around them and anything she could think of, the therapist worked toward one goal: helping Lucinda develop logical thinking processes.

4. LD therapy is done individually or in very small groups. One of the reasons for this is that no two learning disabilities are exactly the same. For example, a child who has a problem with visual memory needs therapy that is different from that needed by a child who has difficulties with auditory memory. If the two children are plopped into the same class, things don't work out too well.

Brad had an unusually weak auditory memory. He could not remember even a simple four-word sentence unless it was repeated several times. As part of a group of seven sixth-graders, he had a horrible time with dictations.

If I dictated a ten-word sentence by reading it twice, the rest of the group would carry the whole thing in their heads and write it down from memory. But Brad would be lucky if he could remember the first three words.

There was no way to adjust to Brad's needs without either embarrassing him or distracting his classmates. He should have had the intense special help possible through one-to-one therapy.

An LD child needs to work in very close contact with his teacher. In a room full of other children, his learning disability makes it impossible for him to work independently for more than five or ten minutes. (Young children cannot work alone for that long.) If he is left on his own, his attention drifts off, his mind wanders, and he slips into daydreaming or horsing around.

Close contact is also necessary as a way to guard against a build-up of frustration. The LD child becomes frustrated very easily. When he gets stuck on a word or question, he needs help right away. His frustration builds quickly to the boiling point. If it takes his teacher a few minutes to get to him, he'll become too angry and discouraged to get back to work. A group of six or fewer students allows for the kind of close contact needed for successful LD therapy. Given the right group, a sharp, energetic specialist can maintain the necessary level of close contact with as many as ten students. But in a group of more than ten, that important part of good therapy suffers terribly.

LD children are easily distracted. The least little noise or movement will break their concentration. Even in the ideal situation, their attention span tends to be very short. The normal activity in a room of thirty students is more than they can handle. They simply cannot tune out the many small distractions created by a large class. They need the kind of controlled, quiet atmosphere possible only in a very small class.

LD classes are usually full of boys. And boys will be boys—learning-disabled or otherwise. Little boys tend to be wiggly, loud, rough, and playful. LD boys are even louder, rougher, and more wiggly. Many of them are hyperactive. Some are very hot-tempered as well.

LD children (especially those past the age of ten) often have a long history of behavior problems. Temper tantrums, tears, fist fights, sulking, destruction of property—all are common. After years of failure and frustration, LD children are full of anger. And they are quick to show it. A class full of such students puts terror into the hearts of all but the bravest teachers. Six are a handful. Ten can usually be kept under control by an experienced professional. Fifteen or more are physically dangerous to the teacher, the building, and each other.

My fifth- and sixth-graders were cleaning up after an art lesson. Each of the ten boys had a particular task. Moving furniture back into place, putting away glue and scissors—everyone was doing his job. Except Ted.

Ted was supposed to be gathering up leftover tissue paper that was good enough to save for future use. Instead, he stood around idle while everyone else worked.

At first I ignored his loafing on the theory that he'd get started on his own. When that didn't work, I tried a few gentle hints.

Ted was in a rotten mood. He snatched up the bag he was supposed to be using and stomped over to one of the big tables. Instead of starting in a spot where no one else was working, he walked right into Tommy. Ted was a big boy. The smaller ones were all afraid of him. But Tommy was big and tough. He stood his ground. Ted grabbed him by the shoulders, shoved him aside, and shouted right in his face, "Move over!"

Surprisingly, Tommy didn't come out slugging. He clenched

his fists for just a second, then calmly moved to another part of the table.

I tapped Ted on the shoulder. When he looked at me, I said firmly, "That was rude."

He slammed his bag down on the table, folded his arms across his chest with a "humph," and stared at me with fire in his eyes.

Two of the younger children sized up the situation and acted immediately—one reaching for Ted's bag, one starting to gather up the scraps of paper.

I waved them off. "Don't touch a single piece of that paper. Ted will be picking it up."

"No I won't," Ted snapped, then walked angrily over to his desk and plopped down.

I gave him a minute to cool off, then went over to him. It seemed stupid to make an issue over a few pieces of tissue paper, but Ted was so hard to handle that he couldn't be allowed to get away with *anything*. I simply told him, "The bus will be here in ten minutes."

He stuck out his jaw, narrowed his eyes, and glowered at me in silence. He knew that nobody was ever kept after school. He figured he had the advantage.

A few minutes later I gave it one more try. For some reason I was calm when I said, "The bus leaves in seven minutes. If you intend to be on it, you'll have the tissue paper picked up."

He sat up straight as a ramrod and snarled through clenched teeth, "I ain't pickin' up no paper."

There was no question about it—if I had pushed him any further, he would have exploded. He looked as if he was ready to smash some furniture or take a swing at me. Any real violence would have stirred at least five other boys into action. It could have developed into a free-for-all. With nine other children in the class, anything might have happened. And had something happened, I could not have controlled it. I was not about to let Ted get away with such behavior; I had to stand my ground. But I couldn't risk standing up to him alone.

Letting Ted think he had won, I announced to everyone, "Five minutes until the bus gets here. Anybody who expects to be on it will be in his seat with his job done, coat on, and homework in hand."

The boys knew the end-of-the-day system. Everything was calm. Ted was still sitting rigidly, but he was quiet. I slipped out of the room.

When I got to the office, our principal was at his desk. (We were fortunate in having an exceptionally fine principal, who was usually available and always cooperative.) Without exchanging even a hello, I told Mr. Northrup, "I need you to come up to my room to get Ted." He got up immediately. As we walked back to my classroom, I briefly filled him in on the situation.

When we got there, the boys were all in their seats, talking among themselves. Mr. Northrup walked over to Ted's desk and told the boy, "I need to see you in the office."

Had Ted gotten up and gone with the principal at that point, no one would even have noticed. Instead, he muttered, "I didn't do nothin'."

Without raising his voice or adding any explanation, Mr. Northrup repeated his original statement.

Ted looked at his lap as he replied through pouting lips, "I ain't goin' to the office."

"Yes, you are, Ted. I need to see you."

With that, Ted exploded out of his seat, his face red with rage. "I ain't comin' and you can't make me," he shouted.

Mr. Northrup was not a large man. Facing that out-of-control twelve-year-old, he looked small and helpless. Yet his words and attitude were completely firm and calm. "Yes, Ted. I *can* make you. Now come along with me."

Ted screamed back another round of refusals.

The rest of the class sat watching the scene in stunned silence.

Around and around they went. Mr. Northrup stuck to the one issue as Ted kept refusing to go.

"My bus is gonna be here in a minute. You ain't gonna make me miss my bus."

"I need you in the office."

"You can't keep me after school."

"We need to go to the office."

"It's time for me to go home and there's nothin' you can do to stop me."

"Ted, I'm not very big. By myself I probably couldn't stop you. But I have the authority. I can get others to help me get you to the office."

Although he was still standing there boldly shouting in his fury, Ted suddenly seemed to realize that he had lost. "Okay. I'll pick up the paper."

"No, you'll come with me to the office." Mr. Northrup was superb. Arguing with him seemed about as pointless as fighting the law of gravity. Ted finally realized that and went off peaceably with the principal.

It is impossible for a teacher to maintain control over large groups of LD children. If an adult does not have complete control, a child like Ted can be very dangerous—and among LD children, there are many who are like Ted. For the safety of everyone concerned, LD classes must be kept very small.

## Good LD Therapy

To achieve any good results at all, LD therapy must be done systematically and consistently. Whether working with groups or individuals, the LD teacher needs to spend between three and five hours a week with each student. That time should be divided into equal sessions of no more than 1½ hours each. Sometimes, however, it's necessary to squeeze all the instruction into one large lesson per week. That can work, but it has *serious* disadvantages. And except in a few special situations, if therapy is done for less than a total of two hours per week, it can do more harm than good.

When a good therapist works regularly with an LD child at least two or three times a week, progress should be seen within six months.

The first improvement almost always comes in the area of the child's attitude. Parents often report with delight, "He's happier than we've ever seen him" or, "Things are so much better at home. He doesn't have tantrums anymore" or, "He's started doing his homework. We don't have the fights we used to have every night trying to get him to do his schoolwork."

LD therapy does *not* work directly in the area of counseling. Yet, as a result of therapy, students usually become more cooperative at home, more confident of themselves in dealing with others, and more interested in the world and the people around them. A new basic contentment begins to emerge.

If that improved attitude is not seen in the first six months of therapy, then something is wrong. Sometimes the therapist is not suited to the particular child or her methods may not be appropriate for the child's problems. Or it may be that the child is so severely damaged emotionally that it will take as long as a year to get him to put forth any real effort. (That is often the case with older children.)

Good therapy does sometimes produce miracles. But those miracles take time. They rarely happen in less than forty or fifty hours of work. Most of them take considerably longer.

By the end of the first semester of work, there should also be a definite improvement in the areas of the child's disability. He should have reached several important goals in working to improve his skills in reading, writing, spelling, math, or whatever. But those improved skills will probably not carry over into the rest of his schoolwork until later. After one semester of therapy, his regular classwork may be better because of his improved attitude and renewed interest—but the weekly spelling test will still be a horror, the social studies book will remain unreadable, and the grades on the report card will be basically the same. Gradually, through the second semester of therapy (and into the third and fourth semesters, if needed), the regular schoolwork should begin to improve. If, at the end of two years of intensive LD therapy, the child is still not able to function successfully in the regular classroom—it's time to change tactics.

Two years of LD therapy is enough for one child with one teacher using one method. After that, it's time either to back off and let the child try it on his own or to find new alternatives. Those alternatives might include a different type of class or school or therapist, a different set of adjustments within the regular class, a new opinion from another professional, or just a pause to take a breather.

For older children, the results of therapy are much harder to predict. An eager teen-ager can make incredible progress in one month; an unmotivated youth of the same age might make no progress at all in an entire year. Among junior- and senior-high students, great miracles and dismal failures are somewhat common.

So, to state a general rule: Parents should not expect to see progress from LD therapy in less than six months, and in most cases therapy should not be continued for more than two years.

## Once Around Isn't Always Enough

LD children learn well while they're having therapy. Since they do not learn effectively by regular classroom methods, their learning takes place in spurts. When they're not in the process of therapy, they tend to coast until they fall behind.

A third-grader who has had successful therapy will be reading at about grade level, and often above. When therapy is stopped, the child gets along fine with the help of a few adjustments. But since he doesn't learn in the same way other children do, his skills don't improve along with those of the rest of his class. He gradually slips behind. In the fourth grade he may be terrific, in the fifth grade he may start to struggle, and by the sixth grade he may begin to bog down.

The child probably will not need to be given intense therapy again. He already has the skills of grades one, two, and three. He needs a therapist to teach him the skills of grades four and five. It's not that the child can't read: it's that he needs to catch up.

For some children that does involve another long, tough, two-year fight. For many it does not. Usually the desired gains can be made in forty or fifty hours during a summer session, or in three hours of work a week for one or two semesters. In some cases one hour a week for a year may even be enough.

A child who has had successful LD instruction as a youngster should definitely head right back to the same therapist for his catch-up course. If it's not possible to work with the same person, every effort should be made to find a therapist who uses the method that worked before. Once you've found an approach or method that works for a particular child, stick with it!

Some children need as many as three or four rounds of therapy between grades one and twelve; a few get by with having therapy just once. The younger the child is when he begins his first program of therapy, the better the chances are that he will not need to return later for more help.

LD children who have successfully completed their therapy should be tested every year or so to be sure they're not falling behind.

### How Good Is Good Enough?

Some children take a break from therapy even though they're not yet learning as well as they should be. Others are able to reach the point where they are working at a level in keeping with their mental capacity. When a third-grader of average ability is doing average third-grade work in the area of his disability, he's had enough therapy.

Scores on intelligence and achievement tests aren't always the best way to decide if it's time to quit therapy. When a child is happy with his own level of skill, when he finds his level of achievement satisfying—that's enough. The grades on his report card are not the true test.

When the LD child gets to the point that

he has more successes than failures;

he can do most of his schoolwork by himself;

he lives comfortably with his weaknesses;

he feels good about himself; and

he is leading a normal, happy life,

he's in great shape!

## Some Parents Are Never Satisfied

Brenda was a mildly LD child of average intelligence. Unfortunately, everyone else in her family was unusually smart. Her older brothers and sisters were honor students. Her father was a brilliant doctor. When compared with everyone else in her home, that sweet, attractive, hard-working little girl didn't measure up.

After a year of therapy, Brenda was getting average grades in a high-powered private school program. By public school standards she was working above grade level. It would have been unfair to expect more from any child of just average mental ability.

Brenda's teacher and I agreed that the child was no longer handicapped by her mild learning disability. It was time to stop therapy. We believed that her work was absolutely the best that could be expected from a child of her ability.

When told the news, Dr. Wolfe became furious. He insisted that we continue therapy. But our strong, well-informed headmistress supported us when we refused.

We tried to get the doctor to understand that he was expecting more than his daughter was able to give. All his pressure for better grades was making a nervous wreck out of Brenda. She chewed her nails, worried, and was not able to relax. She rarely enjoyed herself as the other children did.

The father insisted that he realized that Brenda was not capable of the great work produced by his other children. But he thought we were wrong in believing her grades were good enough. "Anybody can make Cs," he protested. "With a little more effort, she could make Bs." He claimed he would ease off on the pressure when Brenda brought home mostly Bs!

The head mistress, the teacher, and I pleaded for Brenda for more than two hours. We insisted heatedly that since Brenda was already a slave to her schoolwork, the pressure to get Bs— even if she could manage it—would be too great.

Our passionate pleas had no effect. That brilliant man could not see the damage he was doing.

Parents often have great difficulty accepting the truth about their child. Just as the Lord makes little pine cones and big ones, children are given different amounts of mental horsepower. No parent wants his own child to have below-average intelligence. Many can't even be content with average mental ability. But parents damage their children when they fail to accept them as they are.

LD experts occasionally see children who have been dragged from one specialist to another for repeated testing. Conversations with the parents of those children quickly reveal that the test results have always been basically the same—and always unacceptable to the parents. Rather than deal with the possibility of mental retardation or emotional disturbance, the parents continue to seek a diagnosis that labels their child as learning-disabled. (While the idea of a learning disability would be tough to accept, it is one they could live with.)

Parents who cannot face the real cause of their child's learning problems tend to push the child to achieve the impossible.

And in their panic they spend dollar upon dollar trying to find someone or something to help—tutors, therapists, special schools, mail-order teaching materials, exercise, or strange diets. These merely put more pressure on the child.

Great emotional damage is done when a child feels that even his best is not good enough.

### How to Tell If You're Getting Anywhere

Learning-disabled children are starved for success and praise. Good therapy helps the LD child recognize and take pride in the real gains that he is making. But children respond to the progress they make in different ways. Some youngsters will rush home to tell all about a new skill they've mastered; some won't.

If the child's attitude and behavior are improved, if he seems happier and more confident, it is safe to assume that he is learning successfully whether he talks about it or not. Don't pressure him to tell you what he has learned. Ask his therapist. And don't settle for vague non-answers such as "We've been working to improve his auditory discrimination." Get the details about exact skills being mastered: "He's learned to write the cursive letters from *a* through *m*" or, "He's learned to find the main idea in a simple paragraph" or, "He now can write one good complete sentence with a capital letter and correct punctuation." Be careful to recognize the difference between important skills and "therapeutic techniques." The therapist may show parents some papers and explain, "We're working to improve pencil control. See how much better he's gotten at making nice, round circles and straight, even-slanted lines? Notice how he can now trace these patterns without going out of the lines." Parents should realize that such exercises are important in helping the child overcome his disability. But the crucial question to ask is, "How's his handwriting coming?"

If the specialist says he has learned to tell a triangle from a trapezoid, everyone should rejoice. But more important is, "Can he now tell an *n* from an *m*?"

LD therapy goes very slowly. There are many, many small goals that must be reached before the major goal is attained. Be sure your child is having success reaching these many small goals. If he is, you know that he is making progress.

> Ted's mother called me one night and said, "Things must be going well. Ted insisted I hear him say his multiplication tables at dinner tonight."
>
> I agreed that he was indeed making wonderful progress in math. "He's learned the tables from zero through five and is very proud of it. For a boy four years behind in math, that's quite an accomplishment."
>
> The woman's delight put a lilt in her voice. "In five years of school, Ted has never come home and told us what he's doing. And now he wants me to buy him some flash cards and practice with him."
>
> That mother didn't need me to tell her. The sparkle of pride and excitement in her son's eyes told her that he was learning and that he was very happy about it.

There are two questions to ask in determining the success of ongoing therapy: Is the child learning real things that are steps toward his goal? Is he feeling better about himself and the world? If the answer to both of those is "yes," then progress is definitely being made.

### Predicting Progress

Doctors, mechanics, psychologists, plumbers, LD specialists —people in the repair business who are paid to fix either things or people—are always being asked to predict how successful their work will be, how much it will cost, and how long it will take. All fix-it people are experts at avoiding giving answers to such questions. "There are so many intangible factors involved," they tell us. "Until we actually open it up and take a look, we can't be certain what we're dealing with." In great, flowing phrases, they refuse to answer the questions of frightened patients, customers, clients, and parents.

That is a cop-out!

No one is asking for a mystical seeing into the future; everyone knows that precise predictions are impossible to make. But any professional who is trained and experienced in his field knows what results can be expected from his efforts. A surgeon might tell his patient that if all goes as planned, the operation will take two or three hours, hospitalization will be necessary for between five and ten days, rest and recovery at home will take three or four weeks, and normal life will be possible again in seven weeks or so. That does not guarantee that the patient will not die on the operating table. Nor does it overlook the possibility of a miraculous healing. It is simply a statement of what will probably happen.

Teaching an LD child is not quite so cut-and-dried as repairing a carburetor or removing a gallbladder. But LD specialists can and should share that same type of prediction with the parents of their students. After testing a child and working with him for a month, the therapist knows what she hopes to accomplish with him in a year. She knows the areas in which her own teaching methods and techniques will be a great help to the child, and she also knows the problems that she will not be able to help him overcome.

LD specialists *do* believe in miracles. There is always the hope that each new student will have the kind of incredible success that happens to two or three children out of every hundred. However, a therapist is also realistic enough to know that a pupil will rarely improve as much as she hopes he will. In all cases the parents need to be told what gains can be reasonably expected from therapy.

There are many different methods, techniques, and approaches in the therapy for learning disabilities. No two are exactly alike. No two can be expected to produce identical results. For instance, a group in Florida is doing some very exciting research in the area of sequencing problems. With their new methods they are having success in helping LD children overcome those problems. But most other experts do not really expect to remedy the disabled child's sequencing trouble; they usually believe that the child will have to live with it for the rest of his life. In response to the question, "Will my child ever overcome his sequencing problems?" the Florida group would say "yes." Until the results of the Florida research are more widely accepted, most LD specialists would say, "No, but we'll teach him to read in spite of it."

Thus, it must be remembered that the progress one can expect to see in an LD child depends greatly on the method used by the child's therapist. There is no one method that always works miracles. There are many methods that never accomplish much at all.

With that in mind, parents can use the "predictions" below as a guide in measuring what they should hope for and expect from their LD child's therapy, assuming that all goes well.

• Parents should hope and expect that the child will learn to read.

To be considered literate, a person must be able to read as well as the average child who has successfully finished the third grade. If an individual reads at or above that level, he should be able to survive. That would allow him at least to read ballots, road signs, applications and forms, letters, part of the newspaper, and a few magazines. It would be rough, but he could get by.

Of all the LD children I've taught, there are only three that I honestly believe will never be literate. No teacher, no method, no amount of time or money is going to teach those boys to read. It does happen; a few children do have a learning disability so severe that they are doomed to be nonreaders forever. But with the right kind of therapy, almost all LD children can be expected eventually to read at least as well as the average fourth-grader.

To predict how far beyond mere literacy an LD child will progress, one must consider the child's particular strengths and weaknesses. In general, the higher the child's level of intelligence is, the higher his reading level will become. And without question, the younger the child is at the beginning of therapy, the better his chances are of overcoming his problem. In the case of older children who've been damaged emotionally, there is no way of knowing what the results of therapy will be. The same applies to young adults who've given up entirely.

• Parents should hope but not expect that the child will become a normal, average reader.

Bright LD children often become good readers; less intelligent LD children often learn to read adequately. But the learning-disabled child seldom learns to read as well as non-LD individuals of the same age, intelligence, and education. An eighteen-year-old high school graduate with an IQ of 140 should be an excellent reader. If that person is learning-disabled, he'll probably just be better than average at reading. Either way, he can get through college. If he is learning-disabled, he'll have to work harder.

No matter how smart the person or how successful the

therapy, most of the learning-disabled will always be slow readers. They may become skilled enough to read accurately and to understand anything they see, yet they continue to feel frustrated that it is impossible for them to learn to read rapidly.

Children with disabilities in areas other than reading, writing, and spelling sometimes become excellent readers. That is often the case with bright children who have expressive problems, writing disabilities, or both.

Many individuals with reading disabilities never overcome their dislike for reading. Yet, even among those who will always read poorly, some do, as adults, develop a love for reading. Bright children with writing or math disabilities are often avid readers from a very early age.

• Parents should not hope or expect that the child will ever become a good speller.

I have never seen an LD person who became a "good" speller. A few learn to spell adequately. Most must rely on secretaries, friends, spouses, or the dictionary throughout their adult life. Fortunately, that is not a particularly great handicap to most adults.

• Parents should hope and perhaps expect that the child will learn to tell right from left.

Almost all LD people eventually learn to tell one direction from the other. Many, however, never overcome their directional confusion completely. Through the use of memory tricks they learn to compensate for their inability. But most are never able to distinguish right from left quickly, easily, or automatically.

• Parents should hope and perhaps expect that the child will not always feel inferior.

The older a child is before being identified as learning-disabled, the more likely it is that he will never lose his emotional scars and feelings of inferiority. Little first- and second-graders who are recognized and helped early often develop no feelings of inferiority at all. Children who struggle through six or more years of failure and frustration have a poor chance of ever getting over the feeling that they are stupid and worthless.

Love, understanding, patience, honesty, and still more love can sometimes accomplish what at first seems impossible. Even the most severely damaged LD adults and teen-agers are occasionally freed from their anger, guilt, and shame. At times professional counseling helps. Sometimes counseling is absolutely necessary in order to get an individual straightened out enough to function on his own.

• Parents should hope and expect that the child will be able to go to college or trade school.

Whether an LD child continues his education beyond high school depends as much on the nature of the child as it does on his learning disability. A very bright LD child who becomes discouraged easily will not be as successful in college as a less intelligent LD student who is full of confidence and determination.

Four factors determine how successful an LD student will be in college: intelligence, disposition, motivation, and the field in which he chooses to study.

There are many fields in which a learning disability is not a particularly serious handicap to a student. For those with the intelligence and stamina, it is even possible to complete studies in law and medicine.

When guiding young LD children, the two extreme attitudes about higher education should be avoided. A youngster should not be brainwashed into thinking that college is absolutely necessary for survival. Nor should he be told that his learning disability makes attending college an impossibility. The severely disabled and those with only average intelligence should not be pushed toward a college education if they don't freely choose it for themselves.

• Parents should hope and expect that the child will be able to live normally as an adult.

There is absolutely no question about it—learning-disabled adults can live perfectly normal lives. They work around their weaknesses just as everybody else does. If their spelling is poor, they avoid jobs as secretaries and use a dictionary often. If they have trouble with math, they keep calculators handy. Welders, pediatricians, mechanics, architects, lawyers, teachers, coaches, business executives, athletes, sculptors, carpenters, nurses, housewives, engineers, musicians, salesmen, plumbers, judges—successful people with learning disabilities are everywhere.

# TESTING:
## How to Play the Numbers Game

### Getting Your Money's Worth

SOME DOCTORS ASK A YOUNG CHILD A FEW
questions, do a simple test or two, and identify him as learning-
disabled in ten minutes or less. Some clinics take a week to have
a child tested thoroughly by psychologists, neurologists, psy-
chiatrists, social workers, and an army of others. The quick diagnosis is absurd; the extensive team approach is usually not
necessary. Between five and ten hours of testing and evaluation
by a qualified LD specialist or psychologist trained in learning
disabilities is usually adequate to determine whether a child is
learning-disabled.

A good professional diagnosis usually costs *at least* $150.
(Most clinics do not charge for their services in cases of true
hardship.) If the evaluation includes brain scans, interviews,
blood sugar studies, and other tests that take days to complete,
the cost can run into thousands of dollars. However, some learning disabilities are so complicated and puzzling that such an
extensive evaluation is essential.

In this chapter the terms *diagnosis, evaluation,* and *testing*
will be used interchangeably to refer to the process involved in
identifying a child as learning-disabled.

Federal law now requires that all public schools provide free testing for learning disabilities to all students who need it. In spite of that, it remains difficult—though not impossible—to have a child tested at school.

• The red tape is so thick that it is not always easy to prove that a child is in real need of evaluation. But—parents can now expect results if they ask for an evaluation. A written request sent to the child's teacher or principal is usually enough to start the process.

• School psychologists are so overworked that it takes forever to get an evaluation done. But—some states have new laws that force schools to complete diagnoses within very rigid time limits. They usually allow between thirty and sixty days. That is somewhat slow, but certainly reasonable.

• Most school psychologists have very little practical knowledge about learning disabilities. But many of them are becoming increasingly skilled at recognizing and dealing with the problems of the learning-disabled. Colleges are putting greater emphasis on training psychologists in that area of their work

The situation is improving rapidly. Parents should definitely give the school a chance to come up with a reliable diagnosis for a child who has difficulty in learning. If the school's evaluation is inadequate, the parents will have to look elsewhere for testing.

No matter how badly it pinches the budget—the child must be properly tested.

### Get Some Answers

Regardless of who conducts the evaluation or what it costs, a professional diagnosis should answer the following questions about a child who does not learn normally:

## 1. Is the child physically able to learn?

Most children are given routine physical examinations every year. Records from such examinations often contain enough information to answer questions about physical factors that might be preventing a child from learning. (Hearing and vision often need to be checked by specialists. Some children who have 20/20 vision cannot get their eyes to work together, or cannot keep them focused for long periods. Very small problems with hearing can cause big problems in school.)

## 2. Does the child have enough mental ability to learn?

Learning disabilities are often mistaken for mental retardation. Only a good individual intelligence test can definitely eliminate retardation as a possibility in a child who fails to learn. The Wechsler Intelligence Scale for Children—Revised (WISC-R) and the Stanford-Binet Intelligence Scale are the best instruments for testing mental ability (see p. 149). There are other individual IQ tests that are adequate, but no one of them should be trusted to supply a true measure of the child's mental capacity.

Some psychologists believe in telling parents the child's actual IQ score; some do not. Either way, a number or set of numbers is not enough. Parents should be given a detailed explanation of what the intelligence testing revealed. They definitely need to be told the "range" of their child's mental ability.

## 3. Is there an emotional problem that prevents the child from learning?

Most psychologists give a few tests to be sure that a child's basic problem with learning is not emotional. However, such tests are not always administered as part of a routine evaluation.

In any case, the specialist conducting the other tests will be alert to signs that might indicate an emotional disturbance. Most LD specialists are not qualified to test for emotional problems—but they are trained to recognize symptoms of those problems and to refer the child to a psychologist for examination if there is any cause for concern.

If the diagnosis does not mention the child's emotional health, the parents should ask whether there is any sign of a psychological problem. A "yes" answer should not strike terror into the heart. Almost all older LD children are emotionally damaged. The important questions are these: Is he so severely disturbed that he can no longer be reached? Did a psychological problem cause his learning failure in the first place?

### 4. How much has the child learned?

Grades on a report card are not enough to tell what a child has or has not learned in school. In evaluating a child who has trouble learning, standardized achievement tests are absolutely essential to determine exact grade-level scores in silent reading comprehension, silent reading vocabulary, and silent reading speed, oral reading, word recognition, spelling, and math. Many other areas can be tested, but those seven must almost always be checked. (See p. 142 for an explanation of standardized tests.)

### 5. Is the child learning-disabled?

A specialist trying to determine the cause of a child's learning problem should always test for the symptoms of learning disabilities that are discussed in Chapter 2. In addition, the specialist might have the child produce a sample of his handwriting, a simple drawing, a paragraph he creates and writes himself, or some copying work. A visual/motor perception test is also usually a part of the evaluation.

In any case, there should be *some* testing designed precisely to answer the important question: Is the child learning-disabled?

## 6. What kind of learning disability does the child have?

Knowing that a child is learning-disabled is not enough; the exact nature of his disability must be determined. Fancy names are not necessary. What parents need is a full explanation of the areas in which the child is handicapped, as well as knowledge of the areas in which he has no learning problem. The parents, the teacher, and the LD therapist must have that information to guide them in working with the child.

Unfortunately, experts often have a difficult time explaining this part of a diagnosis to parents. Few doctors and psychologists are able to present their test findings in words that parents can understand. (Pediatric neuropsychologists are best at talking to each other. Some are almost entirely incapable of communicating their findings to anyone outside their narrow, highly specialized field.)

Nevertheless, parents should keep asking questions—some of which may seem foolish—until they get answers that make sense to them. Technical language sounds impressive, but parents need a translation into standard English.

## 7. What kind of therapy does the child need?

The original evaluation of a child's learning problem should include recommendations for the kind of therapy the child needs. Those recommendations should serve two purposes. The parents need specific names and addresses of several specialists who can provide the type of instruction the child will find most helpful; and the therapist needs guidance in planning a program suited to the child and his particular disability.

## 8. Given the child's special needs and abilities, what school is best able to help him?

Public school psychologists hesitate to suggest that a child could be served best by some private school; LD specialists at independent and parochial schools are reluctant to advise that a child would be better off somewhere else; and many specialists do not want to go out on a limb and name names of schools at all. Getting opinions about schools is a tricky task, but it must be dealt with. Parents need to be given exact recommendations concerning what school would be most helpful to their child.

Parents should ask four kinds of questions as they go about choosing a school for their LD child: (1) What type of school would be best? Does the child need to be challenged by a high-powered preparatory school? Would he work best in a relaxed and more flexible atmosphere? Would a special low-level program for slow learners be good for him? (2) Which local schools offer the kind of program and atmosphere the child needs? (3) Is there a particular class or teacher that might work wonders for the child? (4) Is a special school for the learning-disabled necessary? If so, which one?

Larry was a fifteen-year-old nonreader. There was not a single school in town in which he could learn at all. But his parents could not afford to send him to a special boarding school.

The psychologist who had tested Larry came up with a solution to the problem. She helped the parents make these arrangements: First, she convinced the state's educational authorities that Larry should be allowed *not* to attend school for the rest of that year. Second, she got Larry started at once on a good program of therapy with an LD specialist. Third, she found ways to get the cost of the therapy down to a level the family could afford. Fourth, she joined the parents in fighting for money from the state to pay for Larry to attend a special school the following year. Fifth, she guided the parents in selecting the special school that would best fit Larry's needs.

Less than six months after his disability was diagnosed, Larry was attending a fine private school for the learning-disabled.

This case is not really unusual. Good psychologists often become deeply involved in helping parents fight for the best school placement for their LD child.

The question of which grade the child will enter is no less important than the question of what school he will attend. A few LD specialists do not believe in having a child repeat a grade, no matter what the situation. A few others are very quick to suggest that a student be held back. Most see retaining a child as an action that can be helpful in some cases.

Repeating a grade must not be viewed as punishment. "You messed up the first time so now we're going to make you do it again!" is *not* the proper attitude to express to the child. Unless letting him try a grade again will increase his chances for success, retention is pointless.

After one year of therapy in my self-contained LD class, Doug was ready to try his hand in the regular classrroom. As a twelve-year-old with a September birthday, he could have been either an extremely young sixth-grader or a slightly old fifth-grader. He was small for his age, and his reading skills were at the high fourth-grade level. We decided that he was ready to succeed as an average student in a regular fifth-grade class.

Doug was not thrilled with the decision. He was in his sixth year of school and wanted to be in the sixth grade with all his friends. We sympathized, but put him where we felt he belonged.

Under the supervision of an especially outstanding teacher, Doug positively blossomed in the fifth-grade class. By Christmas he was the top math student in his room, was doing satisfactory work in all his other subjects, and was happy as a clam. He was definitely in the right place.

Sometimes a child needs to be held back a year so that he can "catch up with himself." Sometimes another year in the same grade would make matters worse. As part of his diagnosis, a specialist should state very clearly his opinion concerning the grade in which a particular child should be placed.

### 9. How should parents deal with the child and his problems at home?

A happy, healthy life at home can be the key factor in helping an LD child. Yet parents usually moan, "How do we live with that kid? Our family life is a mess."

Parents need guidance with questions of discipline, curfews, chores, homework, recreation, and the like. Does the child need set rules enforced with a firm hand, or is it better to be more easygoing and relaxed with him? What kinds of activities should be encouraged? How much sympathy should he be given because of his disability? What should the other children in the family be told about their LD brother? Should Aunt Maude be told? What about the kids in the neighborhood?

More than anyone else involved, the parents need help with those matters. And the specialist who makes the diagnosis is the ideal one to provide that help.

### 10. What does the future hold for the child?

Making an educated guess about what the future holds in store for a patient or student is a routine part of any evaluation.

Once parents know what their child's problem with learning is, they need to be told what to expect. What are his chances of overcoming his disability? Are there more problems ahead? Can they be avoided? Is college a possibility? Will his choice of a career be affected?

### The Specialist's Report

Any good professional evaluation of a child's learning problems should answer most of the questions parents will have in each of the ten areas discussed above. When the diagnostic work-up is finished, the parents should be given a detailed explanation of the findings in a face-to-face conference. In that conference, all test results and recommendations should be thoroughly discussed.

Many specialists do a very poor job of explaining their diagnosis to the child's parents. They simply are not able to put their ideas into language that a nonexpert can understand. Many don't have the time for long explanations. (It takes two or three hours to discuss thoroughly all the topics that should be covered.) Parents need not be embarrassed to ask questions during this conference. It is reasonable for them to insist on clear answers to all ten of the items discussed above, in language they can understand.

In addition to having a conference at which the doctor or psychologist reports on his findings, parents should be given a written report that includes all test scores, other test results, conclusions, and recommendations. The report will probably be written in jargon. This should not bother the parents since the report is intended for use by the schools. It is important that the parents have a copy of this report in their possession for use by a therapist if they should call on one, or for use by a new school system in case the family moves to another town.

A final word of warning: After parents have chosen an individual or institution to test their child, they should make sure before setting up an appointment that they're going to get their money's worth. They should not take their child to anyone who doesn't (1) interview both parents as part of the evaluation, (2) spend at least an hour explaining his findings when the tests are completed, and (3) see to it that the child is given a good explanation of his problem.

## How to Get Real Information Out of a Maze of Test Scores

In considering test scores, it must always be remembered

that they tell only how well a child performed at one particular time and place. Had the child been given the same tests one day earlier or one day later, the scores would not have been exactly the same. The specialist doing the evaluation does take that into consideration. Occasionally he will feel that a child's test results do not give a true picture of his skills and abilities. When that happens, it will be noted in the report and an explanation will be added. But professionals are usually incredibly good at getting children into the right frame of mind so that they will do as well as possible on the tests.

### Standardized Tests

Most tests used to measure intelligence and academic achievement are *standardized tests*. A standardized test is put on the market only after years of research, during which the test is given to thousands of different subjects. The scores are then studied and compared to produce a set of *norms*. (Norms are figures that tell how well a typical group of children of the same age performed on the test that was being standardized.) In that way it is determined just how well a child of a certain age and grade can be expected to score.

Those who administer a standardized test are supplied with information, usually in the form of graphs and charts, about the norms that have been established for the test being given. By using that information, one can compare the test results of an individual child with the scores of a huge number of other children of the same age and grade.

For example: Eight-year-old Robert is given a standardized spelling test in September of the year he is in the third grade. It is hoped he will spell enough words correctly to be ranked as an average speller or better. Let's say Robert spells twenty-three words correctly, and the norm charts show that most beginning third-graders get only twenty correct. Then it is known that

Robert is a better-than-average speller. He is a better speller than the typical child at his age and grade placement.

Standardized tests are based on the idea of comparing one particular individual with a large group of individuals, all of whom are of the same age or in the same school grade as the one being tested.

## Standardized Test Scores

The scores on standardized tests have no meaning in terms of "raw" scores that tell how many answers were right and how many were wrong. To be of any value, the raw scores must be converted to either *percentile scores* or *grade level scores*. These types of scores tell how a child's performance compares with that of others like him.

Percentile scores place the child in an imaginary group of 100 typical children who are exactly the child's age or who are in his grade in school. Picture 100 little third-graders lined up against the wall. We're going to arrange these children in order according to how well they did on a standardized test. The norm charts tell us that Robert's score of twenty-three puts him in the sixty-fourth percentile. Starting with the child who scored the lowest and moving across, Robert will be the sixty-fourth child in the line. The 63 children below him didn't do as well as he did; the 36 above him did better. Or, to take it one step further: 36 percent are better spellers than Robert: 63 percent do not spell as well. Robert is not an amazingly good speller, but the standardized test results indicate that he's better than average. Percentile scores tell where a child's performance stands in comparison with that of others.

Grade level scores tell how much a child has learned. They are expressed as decimal numbers and are very easy to understand. The numeral to the left of the decimal represents the grade level at which the child is working; the numeral to the right indicates how many months into the grade the child has progressed.

In the example above, Robert did as well on the spelling test as most children who are in the fifth month of the third grade. So his grade level score is 3.5. Since the test was given in September, when Robert was 0 months into the third grade, a grade level score of 3.0 would be expected from an average speller. Robert, then, is five months ahead of the average child in his class in spelling.

A child who works at the same level as an average student in February of the sixth grade would be given a grade level score of 6.5; a child working at the May, tenth-grade level would be given a 10.8; and so forth.

Grade level scores are especially useful in watching a child's progress. A tenth-grader who scores 2.3 on a reading test is reading at the level of a typical child in the third month of the second grade. He has a serious problem. When compared with the scores made by other students his age, his scores put him way down at the first or second percentile. Almost all tenth-graders read better than he does. If, after a year of therapy, his reading score has risen to 3.9, he has made wonderful progress. He has gained one year and six months in his level of skill. On the percentile charts he would still be classified as a very, very poor reader down near the bottom. The percentile score compares him with other tenth-graders. It helps us remember he's still one of the poorest readers in his class. But the grade level score shows that he now reads almost as well as the average child just beginning the fourth grade. He is a lot better off than he was last year.

## Intelligence Tests

Intelligence tests measure brain power. *IQ test, test of men-*

*tal ability,* and *intelligence test* are interchangeable names for tests that measure mental horsepower. (*IQ test* is the term used most often. The letters stand for *intelligence quotient.*)

IQ tests measure a person's ability to think in areas that would lead to success in school. They tell little or nothing about creativity, disposition, artistic talent, athletic ability, or a host of other factors that make up the personality and nature of an individual. Mostly, an intelligence test score tells how well an individual can reason, remember, and understand. It is supposed to determine how "smart" a person is.

All intelligence tests are standardized. They work by comparing one person's mental ability with the mental abilities of others of the same age.

## Individual Intelligence Tests

Most schools give group IQ tests to all their students as a matter of routine. For this type of test, each child is given a test booklet. The directions are given to the whole class at once. Then each student must read and answer as many questions as he can in the time allowed. Those who can't read well, can't score well. For the average child, the results of a group test are accurate enough to provide a pretty reliable measure of mental ability. Unless there is some special problem, the vast majority of children never need to be given an individual IQ test.

An individual IQ test is more thorough and accurate than a group test. Since these tests are given orally, one-to-one, by a psychologist or other trained professional, they do not require the subject to do any reading or writing. For some children— the emotionally disturbed, the poor readers and nonreaders, the gifted, the learning-disabled, etc.—only an individual intelligence test can be trusted to give a true measure of mental ability.

## Intelligence Test Scores

Intelligence test scores are usually expressed in one of two ways—as a mental age or as an IQ. (Sometimes, but not often, a percentile score is used. As in the case of achievement tests, a percentile score used to express the results of an intelligence test ranks the child in an imaginary group of 100 children.)

A mental age (which is abbreviated *m.a.*) is used less commonly than an IQ to indicate the level of a child's intelligence. The m.a. score works in much the same way that grade level scores do. Two numbers are given, separated in this case by a dash. The first number represents the year of the mental age of the child; the second number represents the month. For example: A child, no matter what his chronological age, who scores as well on an intelligence test as the average child who is nine years, four months old has an m.a. of 9–4. If he scores as well as the average child who is just about to turn ten, his score will be 9–11. If he scores as well as the average child who just turned ten, his m.a. will be 10–0. M.a.'s are read without pronouncing "dash"; 9–4 is read, "nine four" or "nine years, four months."

Mental age scores are useful in that they allow one to compare easily the chronological age of a child with his mental age. A seven-year-old with an m.a. of 10–6 can think as well as most fifth-graders, even though he is only in the second grade. He is unusually bright, and should be working at a level well above that of the rest of his class.

Mental age scores are very helpful in some situations—especially if the child being tested is mentally slow or retarded. But, in general, an intelligence test score expressed as an IQ gives more useful information. An m.a. can easily be converted to an IQ score by, first, changing the years and months in the m.a. and in the chronological age to a decimal system (10–6 would become 10.5 and 7–0 would become 7.0); second, dividing the mental age by the chronological age (10.5 ÷ 7.0); third, multiplying the resulting quotient by 100 (1.5 × 100). The result produced, 150, would be the IQ score.

The vast majority of IQ scores fall between 80 and 120, with a score of 100 being the perfect average.

To be considered as having "normal" intelligence, a person's IQ must be between 90 and 109. Scores between those two numbers are said to fall into the "average" or "normal" range. Obviously, an individual with an IQ down at the low end of the range won't be quite as smart as someone whose IQ is closer to the high end. Nevertheless, all those with IQs between 90 and 109 are said to have "normal" or "average" mental ability.

Since the learning-disabled, by definition, are of at least average intelligence, the IQ score of an LD child will be 90 or higher—and it can be a lot higher.

It will not hurt to mention again what has already been said earlier in this chapter: Some specialists believe in giving parents their child's exact IQ score; some do not. (Federal laws now state that all parents have a right to see any test scores or files concerning their children.) But the exact number that represents a child's intelligence is not at all important. In most cases in which a specialist prefers not to give out an IQ score, parents should not insist.

The range of a child's intelligence is much more meaningful than the actual score yielded by a test. An individual who is "low average" or "dull normal" is very different in ability from one who is "high average" or "bright normal." The chart below should clarify those and other terms used to describe intelligence. Since the words *normal* and *average* are used as part of the labels for three different ranges of intelligence, the terms can be confusing.

| IQ SCORE | IQ RANGE |
|---|---|
| + more or | Gifted or Genius |
| 140 — | |
| | Very Superior |
| 130 — | |
| | Superior |
| 120 — | |
| | High Average or Bright Normal |
| 110 — | |
| 100 — | Average or Normal |
| 90 — | |
| | Low Average or Dull Normal |
| 80 — | |
| | Borderline |
| 70 — | |
| 60 — | |
| 50 — | Mentally Retarded to Various Degrees |
| 40 — or less | |

## Two Intelligence Tests Parents Should Know About

The Stanford-Binet Intelligence Scale, highly respected among psychologists and educators, is one of the two individual IQ tests best suited to testing learning-disabled children. It is designed to give only two scores; a mental age and an IQ. Any specialist who uses the Stanford-Binet to report on a child's ability in each of the different areas of intelligence that are tested must go to a great deal of trouble to do so. However, most psychologists who use the test will take the time when explaining their findings to point out areas of unusual strengths or weaknesses in the child's ability.

Only a registered psychologist is qualified to administer and interpret the Stanford-Binet. Giving the test requires at least an hour, and usually longer. There is no limit to how high the score may be. Any IQ over 140 is that of a genius; but it is possible for the Stanford-Binet to yield an IQ as high as 200 or 300.

The Wechsler Intelligence Scale for Children—Revised (WISC-R) is more commonly used than the Stanford-Binet and is ideally suited to testing learning-disabled children between the ages of 6½ and 16 years. For young children 4 to 6½, the Wechsler Pre-School Primary Scale of Intelligence is used. The Wechsler Adult Intelligence Scale is for those over 16 years of age. Since most school children are between 6½ and 16, we will confine our discussion to the WISC-R. Vast amounts of research have been done on this test; shelves of books have been written about interpreting the scores it gives. When used by a real expert, the WISC-R can provide information that is much more valuable than mere numbers as a measure of mental ability.

The test is so extremely difficult to give and interpret that only a qualified psychologist can use it. It has the advantage of requiring a bit less time to administer than the Stanford-Binet, and the child being tested usually thinks that taking the WISC-R is fun.

Scoring the WISC-R is a very complicated process. The test is designed to yield three different IQ scores and as many as twelve subtest scores. A wealth of information can be gained through the use of this one test.

The twelve subtests that go together to make up the WISC-R are divided into two categories:

The *verbal* tests require the use of language. The psychologist giving the test asks the subject questions; the child must then figure out the answers and explain them to the psychologist. In all the verbal tests, the child has to *say* what he thinks is the correct answer. The *performance* tests do not require the subject to use language. Once the psychologist has explained what it is she wants the child to do, he does his part by arranging blocks or pictures or pieces of a puzzle in the way he thinks is correct. The child may talk as much or as little as he wants; what counts is how he performs in figuring out what to do with the objects given him.

Thus, the WISC-R gives both a verbal IQ score and a performance IQ score. For learning-disabled children, those two IQ scores provide the most important information that can be gained from the test.

Usually, the performance IQ of a child is not much different from his verbal IQ. But the two scores are rarely identical. One of the two—and it can be either one—is typically between three and ten points higher than the other. The differences between the two scores in these examples are common: verbal IQ—82, performance IQ—85; verbal IQ—103, performance IQ—98; verbal IQ—128, performance IQ—134.

A learning-disabled child, on the other hand, often has a verbal IQ and a performance IQ that are greatly different from each other. As in the case of a child who is not learning-disabled, either score can be higher. These sets of scores might belong to LD children: verbal IQ—112, performance IQ—90; verbal IQ—98, performance IQ—115; verbal IQ—114, performance IQ—134. Any time there is a difference of more than sixteen points between a child's verbal IQ and his performance IQ, a learning disability should be suspected. (Caution: When measuring the difference between a verbal IQ and a performance IQ, one should make certain that the scores being compared are expressed as IQ scores and *not* as percentile scores.)

When dealing with a psychologist who does not believe in giving out actual IQ scores, parents should ask, "How big a spread is there between the performance IQ and the verbal IQ?" Any specialist will gladly give that information. (Another caution: Some individuals who are clearly LD do *not* have a difference of sixteen points or more between their verbal IQ and their performance IQ.)

The full-scale IQ is the third most important score given by the WISC-R. It is this full-scale score that tells whether or not a child has average or better mental ability. On the WISC-R, there *is* a limit to how high the full-scale IQ can be. Any score over 140 is fantastic; a score of about 160 is the highest that is possible.

The twelve subtests that make up the WISC-R are divided into six verbal tests and six performance tests, as follows: *verbal tests*—information, vocabulary, comprehension, math, similarities, digit span; *performance tests*—picture arrangement, picture completion, block design, object assembly, coding, mazes.

Few psychologists give all twelve subtests to any one child. The WISC-R is designed in such a way that several subtests can be left out without harming the reliability of the IQ scores that the test yields. Three subtests are often not given: the digit span test (a verbal test) and the coding test and mazes test (both performance tests). The mazes are rarely used, and for LD children that's fine. But the digit span and coding tests can be extremely useful in evaluating the problems of learning-disabled children. Even though many very good psychologists do not normally use those two tests, they, and all the other subtests except mazes, should be given to any child suspected of being learning-disabled.

Psychologists charge at least fifty dollars to give and interpret the WISC-R. The client whose child is learning-disabled does not get his money's worth when any test other than the mazes test is left out. There are a few specialists who give only two or three of the subtests, charge for the full test, and come up with only a full-scale IQ score. To parents who complain that such a procedure is inadequate, those psychologists shout, "Balderdash!" Their claim that a reliable measure of full-scale IQ can be gained through the use of just a few subtests is supported by research. But in using only two or three subtests they're not getting the whole picture of mental ability that is available through correct use of the WISC-R.

### Parents Choose the Specialist; The Specialist Chooses the Tests

There are many fine tests on the market today. Their use allows doctors, psychologists, and educators to study and measure almost everything imaginable that pertains to children and learning. Some are very, very complicated; others are quite simple. And while no two are exactly alike, many are very similar. In deciding which tests to use, each expert has those he prefers above others. Some people like chocolate ice cream, some like strawberry. Some psychologists prefer to use the WISC-R, others like the Stanford-Binet. In *all* areas of testing, it is up to the specialist to decide which tests will give the information he needs and which ones he prefers to use. It is important to realize that in almost all cases there are several equally reliable tests available for measuring the same thing. Two experts may use entirely different tests, yet if they use the tests as designed, they are likely to come up with the same correct diagnosis.

Parents need to understand that experts cannot know beforehand exactly which tests will be used in making a diagnosis. Like a detective, the specialist starts by looking for leads. The information he gains from one test gives clues about areas that need further investigation. Until the snooping and probing actually begin, there is no way to tell which tests will be required or what they will reveal. Some areas of the child's ability will always be tested. Others will be studied only when the need is indicated.

Keeping in mind the basic format of good testing discussed earlier, parents should find a specialist they can trust—then let him do the testing in his own way.

## ·8·

# TYPES OF LD PROGRAMS
# IN THE SCHOOLS:
## Variations on a Theme

THINK UP A FANCY TERM AND EVERYBODY jumps on the bandwagon to try out the new idea. Teen-agers, politicians, and educators are always "into" some new fad. It seems that each year a new craze develops, complete with its own "with it" vocabulary. In the field of education, the last ten years have seen a variety come and go: *new math, team teaching, homogeneous grouping, prescriptive teaching, open classrooms, individualized instruction, mainstreaming.* Mainstreaming hasn't left us yet, but it too will pass. As has been true with educational fads of the past, it is not *the* answer.

The jargon sounds impressive; polysyllabic words in pairs always do. Such high-sounding phrases are fine for college professors, textbook writers, graduate students, public speakers, and school superintendents. But parents and teachers need to talk about *real* situations and *real* children.

At different times and places, each of the "variations" discussed in this chapter has had some kind of impressive name. But the names and labels used to describe programs for teaching LD children are not very helpful to parents. What they need is a basic understanding of what *can* be done within a school to help their child learn.

## The Theme

In light of all that we've discussed about discovering a child's special needs through testing, conferences with teachers, recommendations from psychologists, and a consideration of the youngster's personality—we'd like to think that the school would provide exactly the special program he needs to be able to learn. Unfortunately, that is not quite how it works.

Each school system designs its own program for LD students. Those programs are intended to provide special instruction for children with a wide variety of problems. And the programs are always limited by the availability of money, space, and trained specialists.

But within the necessary limitations, a learning-disabled child should be given the type of instruction that is best suited to his particular disability, talents, and personality. There are several possible variations on this theme of using the school's resources to the best advantage of the child. The trick is to choose one that is both practical and effective.

## VARIATION I

**Nothing is done for the child.**

The child's teacher does not talk about his learning disability. She does not treat him any differently from the way she treats his classmates. The child is not labeled; he is not made to stand out.

That, of course, is not really a variation on the theme of helping the child as an individual. Yet it is alarming how many schools ignore the LD child's problem completely. His learning disability may be so mild that a therapist is not required. Nevertheless, if a youngster has had learning difficulties to such an extent that he needed an official evaluation and it was found that the problem was a learning disability, then he does need some kind of special assistance.

## VARIATION II

**The classroom teacher does the best she can on her own.**

It is possible for a very good teacher to work successfully with an LD student without any outside guidance. But that is likely to happen only in a situation in which the child is mildly disabled and the teacher is unusually creative, intelligent, dedicated and energetic—and has time to spare. A teacher working alone cannot be expected to do much to help a more severely disabled child overcome his learning problem. The best she can do is to avoid hurting him. By adjusting the child's assignments and using some of the other techniques discussed in Chapter 3, she can encourage him to learn as much as possible while helping him avoid emotional damage.

## VARIATION III

**The classroom teacher does the best she can under the supervision of an LD specialist.**

In this type of program, the specialist does not come in contact with the LD child. She helps the child's regular teacher find ways to teach him within the regular classroom. The student never gets any therapy.

When this program works as it is supposed to, much of the disabled child's schoolwork is adjusted to fit his problems and needs. Sadly, it usually turns out that the special materials designed for the child are merely used as "busy work" to keep him out of trouble.

The more severely disabled the child is, the less likely it is that Variation III will help him.

Variations I, II, and III have one fault in common: they rely too heavily on the classroom teacher. In some cases methods that depend so much on the classroom teacher *can* work; in a few cases they *do* work. Most of the time they do not.

## VARIATION IV

**The child is removed from the classroom for LD therapy.**

When this method is used, the child goes to the "resource room" for special lessons with an LD teacher. The therapy may be done one-to-one, but it is usually done in very small groups. The disabled students are not tutored in school subjects or helped to catch up with their reading. They are given highly specialized instruction aimed at helping them overcome their learning disability. Such therapy does not replace the student's regular reading class (or math class or whatever); it is given *in addition* to the regular instruction. An LD child who is given at least three hours of help a week by a good specialist usually makes progress.

## VARIATION V
### (*Variations III and IV Combined*)

**The LD specialist gives the child therapy and works with the classroom teacher.**

When Variations III and IV are combined, great things can happen. The LD student goes to a resource room as in Variation IV. In addition to that, his regular classroom program is adjusted to fit his needs, as in Variation III. If there is an attitude of trust and cooperation between the LD specialist and the classroom teacher, a joint effort on their part can produce remarkable results for the child. For the majority of LD children, such a combination of therapy and adjustments in the classroom is the ideal approach.

Unfortunately, LD teachers often *cannot* work with a student's regular teacher. Three common problems can prevent the two from working together successfully:

1. LD specialists are often assigned to several schools. They almost always have to spend a great deal of time screening and testing children suspected of being learning-disabled. It is also common for them to have too many students, too few materials, and too little time for preparation. Paperwork, reports, government forms, long conferences with parents, school-based committee meetings, placement committee meetings, consultations with psychologists and principals—they have so much to do and their schedules are so tight that they often don't have time to work with a pupil's classroom teacher.

2. School systems have policies that limit the activities of LD teachers. Their territory is clearly defined, and they are not allowed to step outside the area in which they are given authority. One rule is very common: LD teachers are not to become involved with any child who has not been through all the committees and who has not been "officially" classified as learning-disabled. Other restrictions vary. Resource room teachers are often told: "You do your job and leave everybody else alone. Stay out of the classrooms." The teacher of a self-contained LD class is often warned: "Do not touch *any* child who is not specifically assigned to your class."

A good LD specialist tries to work around such regulations by making herself available to help teachers through casual conversations. At the lunch table, in the teachers' lounge—anywhere paths cross—she tries to answer questions and make suggestions to the classroom teachers. Small nonofficial exchanges of information have to be used in place of detailed consultations and conferences. Even those little nonconferences are often made impossible by school policy!

The LD teacher is often treated as "different" from the other teachers in her school. The projectors and special equipment on hand for the regular teachers are not available to her; hers must come from the special education storerooms downtown. The books and materials on hand for the other teachers are not available to her; hers must be ordered from the special education department. Often services and materials available to the rest of the school are off limits to the LD specialist.

The principal isn't her boss. And since she must go to her own special education meetings, she often does not attend faculty meetings in the school where she works. Sometimes the situation is so bad that the LD teacher never even gets to know the rest of the faculty in her own school. She works among strangers. She doesn't have enough contact with other teachers to do much good through casual conversations with them. (The more understanding principals tend to ignore rules that make their special education people outsiders. But in many ways, their hands are tied.)

To start my self-contained LD class for fifth- and sixth-graders, I needed materials.

The principal wasn't supposed to make his regular supplies open to my class. But Mr. Northrup personally took me down to the storeroom. In the large collection of free textbooks provided by the state, I found what I needed for social studies and science. Mr. Northrup called downtown to have them send out some math books that were not kept in our building. And he sent me to the reading coordinator to search for the right reading books.

She wasn't supposed to be wasting her time with special education people, either. But she generously spent several hours working with me. We dug through shelves and shelves of state-supplied reading texts. Try as we might, we could find nothing in her huge selection that would suit the needs of my LD students. None would do at all!

I reported my lack of success to Mr. Northrup. He advised, "You'll have to order some books. Get in touch with the LD supervisor."

And so, caught in the trap of which-budget-will-pay-for-this-one, I began six weeks of being shuffled back and forth. Here's how it went:

[late August]     SUPERVISOR: Can't your principal find you some books?

[early September]     PRINCIPAL: I've checked all the supply areas available to me. Nothing like what you need could be found.

[early September]     SUPERVISOR: Get your principal to order what you need out of his budget.

[mid-September]     PRINCIPAL: Get your supervisor to order what you need out of her budget

[late September]     SUPERVISOR: There is nothing in my budget to cover reading books.

[early October]     PRINCIPAL: There isn't any place in my budget where I'm allowed to take money to buy reading books for special ed. They've got $250 set aside for you to buy materials. Ask them to give you that.

[early October]     SUPERVISOR: I can't release your $250 yet. It's not supposed to be used for reading books anyway. I'm sure if you really looked, you could find what you need down at the main repository.

[mid-October]     PRINCIPAL: This is ridiculous. Order what you need. I'll find the money somewhere.

No principal or LD teacher can totally overcome school policies that separate special education teachers from regular faculty members. The official rules create an atmosphere that prevents cooperative attitudes and good working relationships between LD teachers and the classroom teachers they should be helping.

3. Most teachers do not want "outsiders" meddling in the way they run their classes. There is much distrust of LD specialists because of their lack of contact with the regular teachers. Further distrust is caused by the fact that many LD teachers walk into a classroom and give criticism rather than help. LD specialists are famous for blaming teachers for all of a child's learning and behavior problems. And they are absolutely notorious for coming up with suggestions that are completely unworkable. The problem is that most LD specialists have no experience in regular classroom teaching. They have no conception of what the classroom teacher is up against. When they do walk into a classroom, they cause hurt feelings by asking the impossible.

Good therapy combined with a carefully adjusted program in the classroom is the *best* solution for most learning-disabled students. It is unfortunate that schedules, rules, and a lack of cooperation among teachers often cheat an LD child out of his best chance for real success.

## VARIATION VI

**The child is removed from the classroom for LD therapy and for instruction in the areas directly affected by his disability.**

Some children are so weak in one or two particular subjects that they really cannot learn those subjects in a regular classroom. When a student has no chance for success in a given subject, he should be removed from the classroom and the subject should be taught to him by a specialist. In this type of program, a child with a math disability, for example, would never be a part of the regular math classes. All his math would be taught to him by an LD specialist. Such a program is most often used to teach language arts or math.

Classroom teachers tend to like Variation VI because it makes their jobs much easier. In this program, the classroom teacher has to teach only two instead of three reading groups; the LD therapist ends up with the bottom group and leaves the two good ones in the classroom. Also, the LD pupils get therapy without missing a lot of classwork that the teacher must help them make up later. Principals like this variation too. Therapy is easier to schedule if it can simply replace a whole subject rather than being squeezed into some other time during the school day. But the students are often not very fond of such a system. They don't seem to mind being in a special group for instruction, but they often complain because they're not in the "regular book." Not using the same text that everybody else is using leaves LD students open to laughs, teasing, and other "put-downs."

Regardless of who likes it and why, Variation VI is *not* the best method for helping most LD children—though there are some situations in which it is the ideal approach. For "high risk" first-graders and LD youngsters in the second and third grades, Variation VI can work very well.

The Greenway School is a private school designed to meet the needs of average children in grades one through nine. It has an outstanding LD program.

Greenway has a "high risk" program (which is essentially like Variation VI) for grades one, two, and three. *All* children in kindergarten and in the first grade are carefully screened and tested. Those recognized as needing preventive help are put into "high risk" groups at the beginning of the first grade and are kept there until the end of grade three. All their basic language arts skills are taught to them by an LD specialist. They spend two hours a day in very small groups taught with special materials and special methods. Each child is a part of a regular class for the rest of the school day.

As a child enters the fourth grade, his LD program shifts to become much like Variation V. Except in very special cases, the child is a part of regular reading and math classes. If his therapy needs to be continued, the child goes to a resource room. The therapist guides the classroom teacher in adjusting the child's regular work.

The Greenway School's approach to dealing with learning-disabled children is unusual in several ways: (1) LD youngsters are discovered before they have a chance to fail. This means that most of those children do not become freaks with behavior and social problems. (2) The program is flexible. The structure of a child's therapy can be adjusted to fit his changing needs. (3) All therapy is done by highly skilled professionals. (4) Every member of the faculty, staff, and administration is well informed on the subject of learning disabilities. They all understand LD children and their special problems. (5) Classroom teachers work closely with LD teachers in helping the disabled children.

The key ingredient in Greenway's LD program is the high level of cooperation and understanding that exists between the regular classroom teachers and the LD specialists. They work together in an atmosphere of mutual trust and respect.

## VARIATION VII

**The child is given all his instruction in a self-contained LD class.**

Very few children have such a severe learning disability that they can't function in a regular classroom for at least part of the school day. If only for art, music, physical education, and lunch, the learning-disabled child should be given the chance to be with "normal" youngsters.

But there are some LD children who truly cannot succeed

at any of the things done in regular classes. They can't do the classwork because of their disability; they can't take part in other activities because they have such severe emotional problems. They fight, sulk, skip school, cry, destroy things, run away, steal, hide, and keep the whole class in an uproar. If an LD child gets to the point that he can't even eat lunch in the school cafeteria without ending up in tears or a fight, it's time to consider placing him in a self-contained class.

In a self-contained LD class, the students spend all day with one teacher—a learning disabilities specialist. She is the class's only supervisor and she teaches all subjects, usually including art, music, and physical education.

Two types of children need self-contained LD classes: those with a very severe learning disability and those with serious emotional problems caused by their learning disability. (The LD child who quietly fades into the woodwork in his misery is not likely to be placed in a special LD class. Yet he needs it just as much as the ones who break windows and shout curses at the teacher.)

Self-contained LD classes are designed to serve three functions:

1. They provide the LD child with a place where he *can* learn. Because the child is so easily distracted and has such a short attention span, he can work only in a very small class. Because his needs are so special, he is better off in a class with other children who have similar needs. Because he must have so much personal attention and close supervision, he has to have a teacher who has the time to work with him. In some ways he must be allowed extra freedom; in other ways he must have unusually strict control. A small, quiet class with a teacher and classmates who understand his problems will give the LD child a chance to learn.

2. They provide LD therapy. In all the other programs for teaching LD children, it is impossible to give a pupil more than about five hours of LD instruction per week. The student in a self-contained class may get as much as fifteen hours of such work in a week. Since the therapist is always there, every learning activity can be a part of LD therapy. Only huge amounts of therapy will give some severely disabled children a chance to learn.

3. They provide an atmosphere in which the child can learn factual information. The LD child fails in a regular class because he can't read the books. If he's lucky enough to have someone read his books to him, he still can't pass the tests because he can't read them either. In an LD class, the teacher finds ways of getting the information into the student's head. She teaches him the same material, but by totally different methods. The child is in a small class taught by a teacher who knows how he *can* learn. The approach is one of show him, tell him, let him do it and learn from a real experience.

My self-contained class of fifth- and sixth-graders was studying explorers. Because of their learning disabilities, they all had a poor concept of time. There was no way to get them to really understand Christopher Columbus's incredible voyage by simply telling them, "He spent more than eleven weeks at sea." To them, eleven weeks meant nothing.

To get the point across, we elected one boy to be Columbus, and we launched three imaginary ships.

Every day, right after lunch, we had a report from Columbus. Our captain would rise, then make his announcement in a very serious voice: "Today is our thirty-third day at sea. The weather is stormy; the sea is rough. We've run low on water, and some of the crew want to turn back. No land has been sighted." Our Columbus did a great job of coming up with a logical report every day.

The rest of the class loved to grumble and complain about the voyage and the living conditions on the ship. They put their hearts into being a miserably unhappy crew.

Week after week our skipper gave us his daily report as he marked off another day on the calendar.

By the end of the fourth week we were all tired of the whole thing. We were sick of reciting the little rhyme, "In fourteen hundred and ninety-two, Columbus sailed the ocean blue." We were tired of talking about our three ships. We hated to hear the name of the queen who had financed the ghastly adventure. But, like the great explorer we were following, we kept on.

For eleven solid weeks we continued. It nearly drove us crazy!

When land was finally sighted, we were overjoyed. We were so relieved to have the whole thing over with that we had a party to celebrate.

At five minutes a day for over eleven weeks, our class spent about five hours studying that famous trip of discovery. Yet, no historian will ever understand the voyage of Christopher Columbus better than those boys and I do. We learned about it through a shared experience.

The self-contained LD class should be used only as a last resort, after all other methods of therapy have been tried. The student who *can* function in a regular classroom should be allowed to do so.

On the other hand, teachers and parents should not hesitate to place a child in a self-contained LD class if he truly needs to be in that class. Where the student *wants* to be should have no effect on the final decision of where he is placed.

I've never met a child who entered a special LD class on the first day of school looking as if he wanted to be there. Parents and principals drag them in, push them in, force them in. But once those students get there and find out what it's like to succeed, once they discover they're not alone, once they've tasted the feeling of being understood, once they're removed from the teasing and criticism they got from students in the regular classroom—then their parents start calling to say, "This is the first time he's been happy since he started school." Soon the child tells his teacher, "You're the first nice teacher I've ever had." Friends and neighbors notice the difference in his attitude and behavior. A former teacher will stop him in the hall to say, "Oh, Billy, you used to be such a devil. I'm glad to see you doing so well."

A child who truly needs to be in a self-contained LD class will be very happy there—in spite of what he thinks at first.

### And the Bright LD Child Goes Unhelped: Injustice under the Law

The law says that all children must be given a free education appropriate to their needs. State and federal guidelines specify that for a child to be considered learning-disabled, he must be two years below grade level. The laws are set up to help those who would never learn at all if they didn't get special attention. They are aimed at getting help for the children who are in critical condition.

And that's great. Most schools would not do much for learning-disabled children if they weren't forced to do so; history proves that.

But the laws also mean that a whole group of learning-disabled students do not get help in the public schools. Sadly, it is the children with the most potential whose mental talents are allowed to go to waste. LD children with high IQs seldom get into special LD programs!

An LD child with an IQ over 120 can be severely disabled yet still not fall two years behind the rest of his class. He may have a very serious learning problem, but his natural intelligence allows him to do passing schoolwork in spite of it. On his own, he can find ways to work around his disability, compensate for it, adjust to it, and make do. He won't be able to perform as the bright child he is, but he will be able to survive in school.

Look at the figures: A youngster with a full-scale IQ of 125 has a mental capacity that is 25 points higher than that of the average child. He should do about 25 percent better in school. As a fourth-grader, he should read at the fifth-grade level. In the eighth grade, he should be working at the tenth-grade level. If he's doing just average work, he's not doing as well as he should. He is two years behind where he *should* be. And he's frustrated. He's just as frustrated as some eighth-grader of average intelligence who is working at the sixth-grade level. In fact, he is probably more frustrated.

He feels that something is wrong. But nobody will listen. He knows he's having difficulty, but the adults in his life will not take his complaints seriously. He is particularly likely to get lectures about not putting forth enough effort, not really tuning in and paying attention, or not being organized or disciplined enough. He will probably be blamed rather than helped. That very bright child is headed for serious trouble.

> Thirteen-year-old Raymond came from a prominent family and attended the most respected private school in town. Usually quiet and gentle, he had always had a flashy temper. People thought he was a bit odd. But he was not a troublemaker or a "punk."
>
> When he was in the seventh grade, Raymond got into trouble for theft. After he had been caught, it was discovered that he would steal anything that wasn't nailed down.
>
> Raymond was not treated as the juvenile delinquent that he appeared to be. Instead, he was taken to a psychologist for testing. His parents hoped that the cause of their son's antisocial behavior could be determined.
>
> The testing revealed two important facts about Raymond: He was extremely bright, and he was learning-disabled. He had man-

aged to learn to read and do math well enough to get by all right in school. But even his high level of mental ability was not enough to make it possible for him to overcome his weaknesses in spelling and writing. He could do all his other school work successfully. But with a pencil in his hand, he fell apart!

Raymond was lucky. His parents were interested in his problem, and they had the money to provide him with testing and therapy at a clinic. His private school cooperated by adjusting his work and his schedule. Raymond got the help he needed—and certain disaster was avoided.

If Raymond had been in a public school, he would *not* have gotten therapy. (He probably wouldn't even have been tested.) His parents would have been told, "Look at his grades. He's doing average work in everything but spelling—he's not learning-disabled." Or they might have heard, "Yes, he is learning-disabled, but since he's not two years below grade level, we can't place him in any of our LD programs. His problem is so mild—he's getting along fine."

That is where the law begins to work against the bright LD child. Even when a public school does want to help him, the law makes it impossible. School officials shrug their shoulders as they turn desperate parents away. "Sorry," they say, "but we have to abide by the guidelines. Unless a child is two full years below grade level, we can't touch him. . . ."

Guidelines—poppycock! The guidelines must be changed. The law should read that no child gets help unless he is working "two years below *his potential*" instead of "two years below *grade level.*" The present wording discriminates against bright children! *Any* child who is performing in school at a level two years below his ability is disabled enough to need help.

I was introduced to Barbara at a club meeting. When she learned that I was an LD specialist, she told me about her son. Carl was in junior high school and was having serious difficulties. His story was almost identical with Raymond's—except that Carl's behavior problems had not yet gotten him into serious trouble, and he was in a public school.

The schools had refused to test Carl for a learning disability on the ground that he wasn't working two years below grade level. So his mother paid to have the testing done at a private clinic. The tests showed that Carl was definitely learning-disabled. He had a very severe writing disability. He also had a very high IQ.

Even when faced with the test results, the schools still refused to provide Carl with any therapy. Barbara tried everything she could think of to find help for her son; she didn't give up easily. But the answer was always the same: "No—he's not two years below grade level."

In her desperation, Barbara asked me what she should do. I had only two suggestions: (1) Fight against laws that cheat Carl out of the education he needs. Write your congressman, the newspapers, the state superintendent of schools. Complain and keep complaining. Scream bloody murder if necessary. (2) Get Carl into the Greenway School. If you can't afford it, remortgage your house. But get Carl the help he needs *now*.

## ·9·

# THE LD CHILD'S ROLE
# IN THE FAMILY:
## Square Peg in a Round Hole?

FIRST AND FOREMOST, THE LD CHILD IS A *CHILD*. He has exactly the same hopes and needs as any other human being of his age. He wants to be warm and fed and cared for. He wants to feel that he's important. He wants to feel happy and safe. In order to live peacefully with others, he needs to learn discipline and responsibility. All children everywhere have those same needs and desires.

Parents would like to be able to give their children the things they need and desire. But no one can give a child happiness; no one can give him a feeling of security; no one can give him a sense of self-worth. Parents can make it possible for children to achieve those ends; but they can never present them to their children as gifts.

It is like the process of baking a cake. You can mix flour and eggs and sugar and milk and so forth. But no amount of effort or determination will turn the mixture into a cake—without the process inside the oven that works magic on the soupy batter.

Raising a child works in much the same way. Parents can provide the right ingredients. But the child must use those ingredients to develop feelings of happiness, security, and self-worth.

## The Ingredients Every Child Needs

**1. He needs love.** From the words, actions, and attitudes of others, a child needs to feel that he is loved. This goes far beyond the simple expression of affection (although that is very important). A genuine interest in a youngster and his activities shows love. A willingness to give him time and attention shows love. The patience to try to understand, the strength to enforce discipline, the determination to teach him responsibility—all the things that are done to help a child develop into the best person he is capable of becoming—all these can be expressions of love.

**2. He needs to feel accepted.** A child needs to feel that those near him think he's okay, even with all his faults and imperfections. He needs to be able to sense that others are glad he's around.

**3. He needs success and genuine praise.** To become a "can do" person, a youngster needs to be successful in at least some of the things he attempts. Seeing his own accomplishments makes him feel good about himself. It helps him develop pride. It encourages him to try other new things despite the risk that he might fail. And the joy of receiving praise at the end of a job well done can make the whole struggle worth the effort.

**4. He needs to be protected.** As much as possible, a child should be made to feel safe. He should be able to trust that others will take care of him when he is not able to take care of himself. From *real* threats to his body, his mind, and his life —he will be protected. But he does *not* need to be protected from situations and experiences that he must eventually face on his own.

At the age of ten, Zeke had been playing Little League baseball for two years. Suddenly, his mother had some doubts. Other mothers didn't let their sons participate because they felt that the children were put under too much pressure.

Seeking an expert opinion, Zeke's mother called the pediatrician. She was given excellent advice. This is the essence of what the doctor said: "Zeke is going to be living in the real world. And in the real world there is pressure to perform. You can't protect a child from life until he's eighteen, then suddenly turn him loose and expect him to be able to deal with reality. Pressure is one of the things that Zeke must learn to deal with. Don't overprotect him. Just see that he isn't put under more pressure than he's ready to handle."

Zeke continued to play baseball every spring all the way through the twelfth grade. He loved it. The pressure was there, but it didn't seem to bother him. He had some great moments of success and some horrible times of failure. He always made the team, but he never got to be the star player.

Some of Zeke's finest qualities were developed through his participation in sports.

**5. He needs freedom to learn and grow.** Children learn from experiences. Parents should encourage their child's natural tendency to be curious and venturesome. They should allow him to discover and pursue his own personal interests and talents. And, equally important, they should allow him to take *reasonable* risks and to make mistakes. The process of trying and failing is part of learning. But in doing those things, parents ought to be careful not to use phrases such as "See, I told you that wouldn't work" or "What'd you try a dumb thing like that for?" when the child does fail. Failures must be expected sometimes and dealt with in an understanding way.

A friend of mine let her teen-age daughter, Marion, drive the family car to school. The girl was supposed to be home in time for dinner at 6:30. At 7:00 she still had not arrived.

When Marion finally walked in at 7:30, she was as pale as a ghost. "I *lost* the car," she gasped. "I parked in the faculty parking lot. They towed the car away. And I can't find out where they took it."

Marion was really upset. She felt terrible for having gotten into such a mess. There was no need for anyone to tell her she had done something dumb. She already knew.

My friend did not get angry at her daughter. Instead, she did what she could to help solve the problem. She made some phone calls and finally located the car. Marion paid the twenty dollars to get the car back. Punishment was unnecessary; the expensive towing fee took care of that.

**6. He needs healthy outlets for his energy and creativity.** Children need to explore and develop outside interests. A child needs free time to amuse himself and play with friends. He must be encouraged to devote time to hobbies and other activities he enjoys. Swimming, rock collecting, scouting, music lessons, raising hamsters, team sports—fun and success in such activities put sparkle in a child's eyes. If a youngster is to become an enthusiastic participant in life, his days must include more than school, chores, and TV.

**7. He needs discipline.** A child needs to live in a world in which there are definite limits on his actions. The "real" world is that way. If you lean too far back in a chair, you *will* fall. That is the law of gravity. "If you play with matches, you *will* be punished." That is one of the rules for a young child. If the rule is absolutely enforced, the child will quickly learn to live within its limitations. The objects of discipline are to keep a child safe and to teach him to be considerate of others. The ultimate hope is that he will develop habits of reasonable behavior and maintain them through self-discipline.

Firm discipline seems to make children feel loved and secure. Youngsters who can get away with almost anything usually feel that their parents don't really care about them.

**8. He needs responsibility.** Children should be taught that they are responsible for their own actions—and that they must think *before* they act. At any age, a child is capable of accepting responsibility for what he says and does.

> A teen-ager caused an automobile accident and was charged with drunk driving. The driver of the other car was killed.
>
> The boy's lawyer, in pleading his client's case, told the judge, "He's young. He used poor judgment. This is the first time he's gotten into trouble for driving under the influence."
>
> The judge's unsympathetic response was, "It was the victim's first time, too."

A child needs to develop another aspect of responsibility as well. If he is not given specific duties for which he alone will be responsible, he will not feel like a full-fledged member of the family. Even a four-year-old is able to clean out the bathtub after himself and to carry out the garbage. A youngster is not his family's servant, but he must not be treated as a guest, either. When a child is given duties that he is capable of handling on his own, he will develop a sense of responsibility and a feeling that he belongs.

In meeting a child's needs, parents supply him with the ingredients that make it possible for him to feel happy, secure, and valuable as a person. Parents do not give happiness itself. All they can do is provide what a child needs so that he can develop happiness within himself.

### Meeting the Needs of an LD Child

The parents of an LD child usually center their thoughts on how he is different from other children. But in doing so, they are starting from the wrong position. They must change their thinking.

A learning-disabled child must be thought of first as a child—

a child with the same basic needs that all children have. His learning disability may become a complication. But the child's basic needs remain the same.

When things go wrong, parents must not look first to the child's learning disability. In dealing with a difficult situation, the first thing to think about is the child's needs as a *child*.

> Bob, who is learning-disabled, starts a fight with one of the children in the neighborhood. If his parents assume that his angry outburst was caused by his learning disability, they will believe it's part of a problem that can't be changed. Therefore, they will either (1) make no attempt to change his behavior at all, or (2) punish him for his bad behavior while ignoring the real cause of the problems. Neither will be effective.
>
> The parents need to shift their attention away from the learning disability and back to Bob's needs as a child. Once they recognize the real nature of the problem, they can deal with it creatively. In this case, the child doesn't feel accepted; he is rarely successful at anything; and he was not protected from the pain of being teased. A logical solution would be for the parents to see to it that these needs are met. Bob should be led to find activities at which he can be successful; guided toward playmates who are not quick to tease; and helped to feel accepted. Then, he won't have such a chip on his shoulder.

Before taking any action to solve a problem that an LD child is having, parents should ask themselves whether the problem is caused by the learning disability or by some unsatisfied need. Very few of the troubles an LD child has are caused directly by his disability. They almost always are a result of the way that he and others respond to the disability.

## Square Pegs in Round Holes

No child fits anywhere until he's *taught* to fit. And a learning-disabled child is no exception.

However, the LD child does have special problems that sometimes make it more difficult for him to adjust to the people and situations he meets. In many ways he is not very different from other children. But for parents, raising a learning-disabled child *is* different.

The traditional approaches used in rearing children simply do not apply to the LD child. Granny's stern philosophy, some of the modern notions of unlimited freedom and self-expression, systems that the neighbors use with their children—they don't give parents ideas that work very well with learning-disabled youngsters.

> Tuesday was Eddie's day to take out the garbage. He forgot to do it. In our society, tradition says that his parents can (a) punish him; (b) bribe him to do better; (c) sit down and have a talk with him, then choose a or b; (d) forget it.

> Tuesday was George's day to take out the garbage. George has a learning disability, and he forgot to do his chore. But none of the ready-made responses that parents usually rely on in such situations is appropriate this time. The parents are on their own.

As problems arise, parents of "normal" children can look to accepted patterns, respected traditions, and their own personal experiences for guidance. From what they've heard and seen, they can choose a solution that should work to settle the matter at hand.

But even when faced with "standard" problems, the parents of LD children have nothing to fall back on for help. What *do* you do when an LD child comes home with three Fs on his report card? Punishing him isn't going to help. He *can't* do much better, so a bribe won't do any good either. Reasoning with him might help a little, but it will not solve the problem. And ignoring the matter will definitely not make things any better. For the parents of LD children, there is no list of tried and true solutions. When traditional methods don't apply, solutions must be *created*.

## Creating Solutions

In developing the ability to create solutions, the parents of LD children must remember that there is never just one way to solve a particular problem. It is never a matter of finding the "right" answer. It is a question of finding the "best" answer. From several possibilities, one should be chosen that seems to be most promising. Again, you're not looking for *the* answer— you're looking for the *best* answer.

The process of creating solutions for the problems of an LD child should always begin with these two questions: What are the needs of the child as a child? How can those needs be met when his learning disability is taken into consideration?

For example, take another look at George, the LD child who could not remember to take out the garbage:

Which of his needs as a child are involved? (1) He needs responsibility. (2) He needs the freedom to learn and to grow. (3) He needs to feel accepted. (4) He needs success and genuine praise.

What aspects of his learning disability are involved? (1) He cannot deal with time; he never knows what day it is. (2) He is forgetful.

The task is to create a solution so that the garbage is taken out and George can have the good feelings of success and recognition that come with doing a job well, on his own. His parents might come up with several plans, some better than others:

Plan A: George's father could take the garbage out on his way to work and save everybody the hassle. But then George wouldn't get responsibility, freedom to learn, success, praise, or acceptance as a regular member of the family.

Plan B: George's mother could put a flag in his oatmeal

every Tuesday morning. That would remind him. But then the garbage wouldn't be *his* responsibility.

Plan C: George could be given the added responsibility of bringing in the newspaper each morning. He could read the day and date off the front page as a general announcement of interest to the whole family. That way he would notice what day it was every day. He would get the garbage out because he'd know when it was Tuesday. Also, he would develop the habit of checking the day and date every morning as a help in working around his difficulty with time. In this way, many of his needs would be met. (What if George announced the day faithfully every morning, but the mention of Tuesday sometimes didn't ring a bell? One of his parents could say, "Tuesday, huh?" as a gentle reminder. If George needed to be reminded every Tuesday, a different plan would be needed.)

Plan D: George could be given his own calendar. At the beginning of every month "George—garbage" would be written in the spaces for all the Tuesdays. Each morning he would announce the day and date to the whole family. As he checked the calendar, he could either remind everybody of scheduled appointments or he could just watch for his own. In addition to having all the advantages of Plan C, Plan D would help George remember his mother's birthday, baseball practice, and his tuba lessons.

The possible solutions for George are endless—right on up to Plan Z, in which he makes a deal with his sister: he takes over her paper route since he tends not to forget things that have to be done every day; he pays her ten dollars a week to take out the garbage and keep track of his appointments for him; and he uses the rest of his earnings to make a down payment on a minibike.

Situation by situation, the possible solutions to the problems of an LD child are always endless. By thinking first of the child's needs as a child, by considering special needs caused by his learning disability, and by being open to nontypical possibilities—parents can find an unlimited number of ways to deal effectively with problems as they come up. There is never just one solution. But the *best* solution can be found through creative thinking and the proper attitude.

## ·10·
# GETTING ACTION:
## Harnessing the Power of the
## Hysterical Mother and Big Daddy

"BACK WHEN MY SON WAS IN THE FIRST GRADE, I knew something was wrong." Mothers of learning-disabled children make that statement with frightening regularity. The child may have gone through four, five, six, or more years of school—suffering and failing. All the time the mother knew something was very, very wrong. Yet nothing was done. In the first conference after an eleven- or twelve-year-old student has finally been identified as learning-disabled, the mother's attitude is usually expressed in a sigh of relief and a tired "Thank God, help at last."

How can that happen? Or, more realistically, how can it happen so often? What keeps parents from doing something? What are they waiting for? Why don't they speak up? And if they are ignored, why don't they shout? A child with learning problems needs very strong support from someone who is willing to take on the whole system if necessary. Usually, that support comes from a hysterical mother.

The hysterical mother could almost be considered a symptom of a learning disability. Hysteria in the mother of an LD child is typical. It's logical. And it can be productive. True, a frantic mother often makes life unbearable for herself, for her child, for her entire family. But the power of the hysterical mother, if used creatively and to its fullest extent, can be very effective in getting help for a learning-disabled child.

## Mothers Do Know When Something's Wrong

Anyone who has spent six years raising a child can trust her own judgment as to whether or not that child is behaving as he always has. If the child has always had a cheerful, happy disposition, entering school should not change him into a whining complainer. Once a father told me that, as a preschooler, his son had lots of playmates and was the wrestling champ of his neighborhood. But after a few months in the first grade, the boy withdrew into a shy, lonely world where he had no further contact with children his age. The parents did not trust their suspicion that something was wrong. They should have. Their son spent fifteen miserable years trying to get through twelve years of school before he finally gave up without a high school diploma.

Educators—teachers, counselors, psychologists, principals, school superintendents—often try to convince parents that there is no way to predict how successful a child will be in school. They tell them, "The fact that your child's achievement level does not meet your expectations doesn't mean something is wrong. The child does not have a problem. You are his problem." In some cases that is true. But more often than not, a mother does have a pretty realistic idea of what her child can be expected to do. From toilet training to bicycle riding, she has watched him as he learned many things. She knows how he approaches a new task, how much curiosity and determination he has, how he handles failure, what he thinks of himself. From firsthand experience she knows whether he's bright or lazy or slow or moody. So, when a mother feels that her child is not as successful in school as he should be, she *is* qualified to make the judgment that something is wrong.

> At the age of three, Charles could name the make and model of every car he saw. But when he was in the third grade, he still could not identify the letters of the alphabet. Obviously, he was not learning to read as well as he should have. His mother knew it. But she didn't do anything helpful with her knowledge.
>
> On a fluke, Charles was identified as learning-disabled by a visiting consultant. At that time he was failing the fourth grade for the second time.

Parents *do* know when something is wrong with their child. No one should be able to convince them otherwise without overwhelming proof.

### Mothers Usually Fail in the First Grade

A mother who knows that her child is not learning as he should—and who is on the verge of hysteria for that reason—usually fails to make creative and effective use of her hysteria. When she goes to confer with her child's first-grade teacher, the teacher offers one or more of these reasons for the child's failure to learn: he's lazy; he's wiggly; he never pays attention; he causes trouble; he doesn't try. Then she tells the mother, "He's just immature; there's nothing to do but wait. Don't worry—he'll grow out of it. Lots of children have these problems. Leave him alone. He'll be fine."

Since the teacher is the expert, since the teacher has so much more experience with children of that age, since the teacher is so sure of herself—the mother makes her first big mistake: she holds back her hysteria. She is calm. She is polite. She forces herself to trust the teacher's judgment rather than her own. She *wants* to believe that her suspicions are wrong, so she goes home to wait and hope.

Most mothers do that; they control their hysteria so that they will not seem to be unreasonable. They do not want to explode. Teachers love them, of course. But little first-graders with learning problems need mothers who explode hysterically from the very beginning.

### The Hysterical Mother in Action

The mother of one of my former students is a particularly good example of a parent who fought for her child from the start. Her son had been in the first grade for only a few months when she became convinced that something was wrong. The boy's teacher insisted there was nothing to worry about. Not satisfied with the teacher's assurances, the mother requested testing. That brought the school's principal into the picture. He refused to request an evaluation by the school psychologist and tried to discourage the mother from pushing the matter any further. Nevertheless, she made arrangements to have her son tested at a private clinic. Unfortunately, the clinic came up with a classic example of a "wishy-washy" diagnosis. Without even using the term learning disability or dyslexia, the specialist recommended a wait-and-see attitude. So, the boy finished the first grade as a nonreader, the family was frantic, and the mother had been labeled a troublemaker.

But this woman was tough. The public schools and a private clinic had not resolved the problem. Next she turned to an independent school. At the admissions interview, she told the director about her child's learning problem. She was told that the school would make its own decision on the matter. After the admission testing was completed, the mother asked that her son be allowed to repeat the first grade. The school placed him in the second grade.

In mid-September, both parents went to confer with the boy's teacher and the school's LD specialist. Everyone agreed that something was indeed wrong. A new evaluation determined that the child was severely learning-disabled. He was given one-to-one therapy, and conferences were held regularly; the solution to his problem seemed close at hand. But he continued to fail in the second grade, and his behavior problems, both at home and at school, were increasing. The frustration that all felt continued to build.

Finally, in midwinter, it was agreed that the boy would be put back into a first-grade class and that the LD therapy would continue. The effect was traumatic for the entire family. Every day the child came home from school crying because his parents had "ruined his life." The mother cried for weeks. She would go into the school's office and sob hysterically. But at home both she and her husband were able to be positive and supportive with their son. It was rough—really rough.

The crisis did not pass until well into the spring. But by the end of the school year everyone was relaxed. The boy was happy —and he was learning. (Three years later his classmates considered him to be the brain of the fourth grade.) Ironically, the child's mother does not seem to recognize the part she played in getting the help her son needed so desperately.

Beginning with the first conference in the first grade, this mother who used her hysteria effectively was the key to finding a solution to her son's problem. She had many chances to settle for defeat; she could easily have adopted the "it's-best-to-be-reasonable" role. But nothing shook her belief that her son could be helped if only she would keep fighting. Her hysteria made her stubborn and unwilling to give up.

Any parent can use hysteria as well as she did.

### The Hysterical Mother on a Budget

Mrs. Williams fought the schools for five years before her son, Ken, was finally identified as learning-disabled and given special instruction. After two very profitable years in a self-contained LD class, he was placed in a regular seventh-grade program—for which he was not ready.

Ken quickly fell back into his old patterns of failure, misery, and anger. Mrs. Williams tried to get her son placed in a more appropriate class. She was given the brush-off by the principal, the social worker, the counselor, several teachers, and a few others.

It was financially impossible for Mrs. Williams to turn to a private school or clinic. Desperate, she called me and begged for suggestions. I gave her a list of people within the school system who I thought might be able to help. She spent another day on the phone. This time she talked to supervisors, administrators, psychologists, other principals, social workers, and more teachers. Some gave her a little sympathy, but all agreed that nothing could be done. There were no LD classes available at the junior-high level.

Mrs. Williams realized that she would *have* to work through the faculty and administration at Ken's school. She had already tried to get them to understand the situation. No one had been willing to listen. But she called the principal again—and demanded an appointment for a conference with all of Ken's teachers. Then she called me and asked that I go to the conference with her. Reluctantly, I agreed.

We were met in the school's library by the principal, fifteen teachers, an LD specialist, the assistant principal, the coach, and a counselor. There were many of "them" and few of "us." If we had thought of that group of people as the opposing team, we'd have been too frightened to say a word.

The principal introduced everyone. Faculty members, teaching aides, and members of the staff—each one of them had *direct* contact with Ken.

Mrs. Williams is a gentle, shy person. In only a few brief sentences and using very simple words, she explained the reason for our visit. The warmth of her personality and the love she feels for her son showed very clearly as she concluded by saying, "We're here because we want to work *with* you."

Since no one at the meeting (with the exception of the LD specialist) had any knowledge about learning disabilities, I began by explaining the LD symptoms that are listed in Chapter 2. To my delight, the teachers were so interested that they took notes. Some of the symptoms were particularly important in understanding Ken's problem. I gave those special attention.

The teachers asked many questions and sought advice from us. They genuinely wanted to understand Ken. They wanted to help solve his learning problems. Long past the time when they would usually have gone home for the day, they kept the discussion going. "How do I treat him?" one asked. "Is he embarrassed about his learning disability, or can I talk to him about it?" Others wanted to know such things as "What kind of work can I expect from him?" "How much pressure should we use?" "What kind of discipline will work best for him?" "What can I do in my class to give him a chance to succeed?"

One by one, Ken's teachers committed themselves to specific plans for adjustments they intended to make within their classes. All that was done voluntarily. Once those teachers recognized and understood Ken's problems, they wanted to be a part of the solution. (From my experience, that is almost always the case. The enemy is ignorance—*not* teachers who don't care. Teachers who truly understand an LD child's situation usually want to do everything in their power to help.)

When the meeting finally broke up, the principal, the shop teacher, and the football coach stayed to talk further. The coach was especially interested in Ken's directional confusion and his poor eye/hand coordination. He'd hoped that the large, muscular seventh-grader would be one of the stars of his team. But Ken's performance had been very puzzling. "He's one of the biggest boys, and he's one of the best players," the coach explained. "But he runs plays to the wrong side a lot, and I can't seem to get him to handle the ball properly. Can you give me some ideas? How can I work around the fact that he can't tell right from left?" Together, we figured out some adjustments that we thought might work. Then the coach realized that he was very late for practice. But he was not concerned. He chuckled as he told us, "Ken is the captain of the team. I don't need to worry about what they're doing out there. He's got them organized and doing their warm-up drills."

Mrs. Williams and I had been at the school for nearly three hours. As we left, the principal shook our hands and thanked us warmly for coming. He asked if I would return sometime and lead a workshop for his entire faculty. After I agreed to do that, he turned to Mrs. Williams and thanked her again. "By coming here to talk with us, you have done me and my faculty a great favor," he explained. "I've been teaching for over twenty years, and I've never seen a child who couldn't tell right from left. I never knew there *were* such children."

We left the school knowing that our visit had done more than just help Ken. In fighting for him, we had also helped stamp out the ignorance that hurts all LD students. Without name-calling or accusations or rage, one mother using controlled hysteria had accomplished some very important things.

A month later, I went back out to the school to watch Ken play football and to find out whether our conference had really helped him.

Mrs. Williams and I huddled on the bleachers yelling, cheering, and talking about Ken. She told me that every teacher had followed through with the adjustments that had been promised. For two or three weeks the school had experimented to find the *best* way to deal with all the different problems involved in teaching Ken. In less than a month he was learning satisfactorily in every subject. His attitude had begun to improve right away. He had quickly returned to his normal, happy, pleasant self.

In fact, life was better than ever for Ken. He was passing all his classes. He was the captain of the football team and had been named most valuable player in three straight games. All the students recognized him as a natural leader. The boys looked up to him and wanted his friendship. The girls stopped him in the hall to talk and flirt. He was very popular with his teachers, too. They admired him for being hard-working, honest, cheerful, cooperative, and well-mannered.

Hysterical mothers don't just get action—sometimes they get miracles.

### Big Daddy: The Ultimate Weapon

Nothing can beat the power of an irate father. When he enters a school to fight for his child, teachers listen, counselors pay attention, principals stand up and take notice. A hysterical mother backed and supported by a strong forceful man—together they make an unbeatable team. The family who has a man leading the fight for an LD child rarely fails!

That seems unfair to the many fatherless families. But it needn't work against them. In my years of dealing with the parents of LD children, I've held conferences with an amazingly varied assortment of father figures: grandfathers, uncles, older brothers, ministers, family doctors. *Any* man standing firmly behind the mother can have a tremendous effect.

A fine private school where I worked had spent two years trying to help Bruce. Yet, at the end of the sixth grade, his situation was worse than ever. The group LD therapy provided by the school was doing no good because the boy's disability was too severe. He refused to cooperate in any attempt to solve his learning problems. He also had serious behavior problems.

Mrs. Miller, Bruce's mother, had been to the school for several conferences. She wanted help for her son. But none of our suggestions to her ever seemed to be carried out.

"What in the world do we do with Bruce?" The school struggled with that question for weeks. The boy couldn't possibly succeed in the seventh grade. He's already repeated a grade; he couldn't be held back again. There seemed to be no choice; Bruce would have to be denied admission for the following year. Any answers there might be for him simply could not be found in our school.

Along with the headmaster, the director of the lower school, and all of Bruce's teachers, I faced the Millers over the conference table. With heavy hearts, we slowly and carefully presented the situation. The conclusion we had reached must have been obvious to the Millers. Mrs. Miller cried softly. Mr. Miller listened in stony silence. Finally, the headmaster took over. As gently as possible, he told them our decision. "Bruce may not return here next year," he announced. The words rang firmly, leaving no room for further discussion.

Mr. Miller was stunned. He did not lean over to comfort his

sobbing wife. For a long time he did absolutely nothing. Then he slowly rose up tall in his chair, leaned forward, and with deep emotion said only one word: "No." There was no anger and no explanation.

The rest of us sat there aghast. Mr. Miller's face and that one word said it all. He was *not* going to let his son be removed from the school.

Then, with the careful control of a businessman attacking a problem, Bruce's father began to speak. "You say my boy has a severe learning disability and needs help you can't give him. What does he need and where can we get it?" he asked.

We recommended intensive LD therapy at an excellent clinic nearby. "Three times a week somebody would have to pick Bruce up at school, drive him ten miles to the clinic, wait an hour while he had his lesson, then bring him back." We told him honestly of the huge sacrifice someone would have to make in transporting the child.

Mr. Miller did not bat an eye. He looked directly at his wife. "It'll be rough, but we'll do it. I'll help out as much as I can. And if we have to, we'll hire a cab."

Having settled that issue, he returned his attention to the rest of us and moved on to the next point. "You say my son is headed into deep emotional trouble. I don't see it. But if you will help us find a good psychologist, we'll take Bruce in for a professional opinion. If counseling is needed, we'll see that he gets it."

No one could argue with that. We discussed the matter, recommended some well-qualified psychologists, and agreed that an evaluation should be undertaken immediately.

Then Mr. Miller faced the last point. "With counseling and LD therapy, can Bruce succeed in the seventh grade here next year?"

Faculty members and administrators agreed completely: "No." The boy was nearly three years behind in every subject. There was no chance that he could succeed in the school's seventh grade.

Not discouraged, Mr. Miller continued. "With counseling and therapy, could he pass the sixth grade if given another chance?"

We agreed that success in the sixth grade was in the realm of possibility—if the therapy went well.

Mr. Miller concluded with this proposal: "I want Bruce here next year, in the sixth grade. We'll get him the counseling and LD therapy he needs. We'll work *closely* with you for one more year. If, at the end of the year, Bruce cannot pass the sixth grade, we'll take him out of the school with no further argument. If he succeeds, he'll stay right here and go on into the seventh grade."

From Mr. Miller's first word, there had been no real question as to whether Bruce would be back the following year. We all wanted to do what was best for the boy. By speaking up, Bruce's father led the school to find a creative solution for his child.

And the solution we found that day worked very well. The last time I saw Bruce he was still at the school, doing satisfactory work in the tenth grade and playing soccer on the varsity team.

I'll always cherish the memory of that father who stood up and said, "No." When the chips were down, he fought for his son. It was a privilege to be a part of such a moment.

## A Long, Tough Fight—Together

It must not be assumed that one success solves all the problems of an LD child. For example, Ken's "miracle," told of earlier in this chapter, lasted for about six months. Then a new difficulty arose. Ken punched a student, was expelled from school for three days, and his mother had to start over. His case is typical.

Each of the stories in this book represents just one episode in the life of a particular LD child; each one tells about a single crisis and how it was resolved. But almost always, one crisis is followed by another. The fight often seems to be endless. As a child's situation changes—as he faces different schools, different teachers, different classmates, and differences within himself—

new problems continue to arise. Again and again the parents must be willing to work to get the help their child needs.

The parents are the key to ultimate success for an LD child. Only they can be counted on to be there, to understand, and to care—day after day, year after year.

Well-informed, forceful parents can give the learning-disabled child his only real chance for success.

# Selected Bibliography

Brutten, Milton; Richardson, Sylvia O.; and Mangel, Charles. *Something's Wrong with My Child*. New York: Harcourt Brace Jovanovich, 1973.

Clarke, Louise. *Can't Read, Can't Write, Can't Talk Too Good Either*. New York: Walker & Company, 1973.

Crosby, Robert M. N., and Liston, Robert A. *The Waysiders: A New Approach to Reading and the Dyslexic Child*. New York: Delacorte Press, 1968.

Ellingson, Careth. *Shadow Children*. Chicago, Ill.: Topaz Books, 1967.

Ginott, Haim. *Between Parent and Child*. New York: Avon Books, 1969.

Gordon, Thomas. *P.E.T. Parent Effectiveness Training*. New York: New American Library, 1970.

Hayes, Marnell. *The Tuned-in, Turned-on Book About Learning Problems*. San Francisco, Calif.: Academic Therapy Publications, 1974.

Kephart, Newell. *The Slow Learner in the Classroom*. Columbus, Ohio: Charles E. Merrill, 1960.

Osman, Betty B. *Learning Disabilities: A Family Affair*. New York: Random House, 1979.

Simpson, Eileen. *Reversals*. Boston: Houghton Mifflin Company, 1979.

Useful Addresses:

ACLD, Inc.
Association for Children and Adults with Learning Disabilities
4156 Library Road
Pittsburgh, PA 15234

The Orton Dyslexia Society
724 York Road
Baltimore, MD 21204

ACLD's in Canada
Kildare House
323 Chapel
Ottawa, Ontario K1N 7Z2

# Index

*Italics indicate case histories.*

Anger, outlets for, 85–90; *Bob, 176; Bobby, 90; Sam, 85–88; Ted, Bobby, and Ken, 89–90.* See also Behavior problems

Attention problems, 39–43, 115–16; distractibility, 40; focusing attention, 42–43; hyperactivity, 40–42; short attention span, 39–40; *Tommy, 41–42*

Auditory problems, 8; *Brad, 115*

Bed-wetting: *Gil, 14*

Behavior problems, 50–54, 107–8, 116; and retrieval, 34; *Berry, 53–54; Bob, 176; Cal, 62–63; Norman, 34–35; Raymond, 168–69; Ted, 116–19; Ty, 54; Walter, 3.* See also Anger, outlets for; Fighting, fair

Bright LD children, 167–70; *Carl, 169–70; Raymond, 168–69*

Children, needs of: in general, 172–75; with learning disabilities, 175–80

Classes, self-contained LD, 12–13, 59–61, 78, 113–19, 163–67; *Ted, 116–19.* See also Therapy

Conferences, parent-teacher, 102–3. See also Parents, and the school system

Copying, problems with, 8, 48

Creativeness, 55–57; *Tommy, 56–57*

Decoding, problems with, 7

Diagnosis, 82; legal right to, 77; symptoms, 19–57; by testing, 133–53; and therapy, 113–14

Directional confusion, 21–22, 43, 130; *Carol, 21–22; Kathy, 38; Ken, 188–89; Ron, 39*

Discalculia, 6–7; *Linda, 6–7*

Distractibility, 40

Dysgraphia, 5–6, 8, 46–47; *Berry, 53–54; Kenneth, 5–6*

Dyslexia, 2–5, 8; *Walter, 3*

"Early intervention," 43–44

Emotional damage, prevention of, 84–92; *Bob, 84; Sam, 85–88*

Emotional disturbance, 11–13, 82, 135–36

Encoding, problems with, 7. See also Expressive problems; Retrieval, problems with

Expressive problems, 8, 49–50. See also Retrieval, problems with

Eye/hand coordination, poor, 8; *Ken, 188–89; Ron, 39*

Failure (of non-LD children): absenteeism, 16; emotional disturbance, 11–13; lack of interest, 17; lack of readiness, 16–17; low intelligence, 8–11; physical problems, 13–14; poor instruction, 15–16; *Gil, 14; Henry, 16; Sharon, 9*

Family trait, learning disabilities as, 22–24; *Bakers, 24; Nelsons, 23*

Fighting, fair, 91–92

Focusing attention, 42–43

Handwriting. See Dysgraphia

Home life, 90–101, 140, 172–80; disruptions, 30–34; *Andy, 36–38; Ken, 32; Matt, 33–34.* See also Homework; Parents

Homework: parents and, 93–101, 108–11; teachers and, 102, 108–12

Hyperactivity, 40–42; *Tommy, 41–42, 56–57*

Intelligence, 8–11. See also Bright LD children; IQ tests

IQ tests, 144–53; chart, 148; individual, 145; and mental age, 146–47; scores on, 147; Stanford-Binet Intelligence Scale, 82, 135, 149, 152;